International
Political Economics

International Political Economics

BRUNO S. FREY

Basil Blackwell

First published in 1984
by Basil Blackwell Publisher Ltd.
108 Cowley Road, Oxford OX4 1JF.

Basil Blackwell Inc
432 Park Avenue South, Suite 1505
New York, NY 10016, USA.

British Library Cataloguing in Publication Data
Frey, Bruno S.
    International political economics.
    1. Economic history——1971. 2. World politics
    ——1975–1985
    I. Title
    330.9′048   HC59

    ISBN 0-85520-748-5
    ISBN 0-85520-749-3 Pbk

*Also included in the Library of Congress
Cataloging in Publication Lists*

Typeset by Katerprint Co Ltd, Oxford
Printed and bound in Great Britain by
The Pitman Press Ltd, Bath.

Contents

Preface

Many students find courses in the theory of international trade to be extremely abstract and to bear little relationship to the real world. This applies in particular to the 'pure' theory of international trade. While the monetary part of international economics is concerned somewhat more with the problems one hears about in the media or reads in the economics sections of newspapers and journals, students are often dissatisfied with the 'pure' theory's exclusive concentration on 'economic' aspects. Being constantly reminded of the importance that politics seems to play in international economic relationships, they would wish to know more about the interaction of economics and politics internationally.

International Political Economics endeavours to provide an analysis of the interplay of economic and political factors in international relations, using the standard tools of economics and of public choice (or of the economic theory of politics). Thus the student of economics is familiar with the tools of analysis here used, and learns that they can usefully be applied also to political aspects of international economics. The approach is based on an explicit theory, but the relationships to practical issues is emphasized by providing *empirical evidence*, sometimes in the form of econometric estimates, but also by way of actual and historical accounts. The reader is not expected to know any econometrics; rather, he is taught how to interpret the results gained by this method. The text is written in as simple a language as possible.

The book is designed both as an accompanying text to a course in the theory of international trade and for students of political science and international relations, who wish to see how the economic way of thinking can be applied to international politico-economic problems.

A first version of the book was written during fruitful and delightful stays at the Institute for International Economics at the University of Stockholm, and as Visiting Fellow at All Souls College, Oxford.

The book benefited much by the comments of my co-workers of many years at the University of Zurich, Dr Werner W. Pommerehne, Dr Friedrich Schneider, Dr Hannelore Weck-Hannemann and Professor Gebhard Kirchgässner (now at the University of Osnabrück). I am also grateful for the help provided in the preparation to my assistants Barbara Gorsler, Reiner Eichenberger and Mico Loretan. Particular thanks are due to Heinz Buhofer, who carefully checked the last version of the manuscript and who helped me in many different ways. I also had the privilege of discussing aspects of my work with the two 'forerunners' of international political economics, Albert Hirschman and Charles Kindleberger. The second part of chapters 4 and 8, comparing competing models of the international political economy, are based on the results of joint econometric research with Friedrich Schneider.

Bruno S. Frey
Zurich, January 1984

1

What is Political in the International Economy?

POLITICO-ECONOMIC INTERDEPENDENCE

After assuming power in 1959, Fidel Castro decided to expropriate without compensation US property valued (by the US Department of Commerce) at $1 billion and to put discriminatory taxes and licences on American products. The United States retaliated by imposing a complete embargo on all trade between the United States and Cuba (except for medicine and food).

This is just one, though spectacular, instance in which international trade and foreign investment were used as political instruments. Indeed, international economics is probably the field within economics in which the interaction between economic and political factors is most intensive. To everyone concerned with such issues, it is obvious that the international economy is strongly influenced by political factors.

Rather surprisingly, however, international economic theory on the whole tends to neglect this interaction between the economy and polity in the international sphere. As one writer puts it, 'Politics and economics have been divorced from each other and isolated in analysis and theory. . . . Consequently, international economy has been fragmented into international politics and international economics' (Spero 1977).

It is sometimes said that economists should stay within their field of study, the economy, and political scientists should stay within their field, the polity. But it is just such a view that fosters the unfortunate neglect of the interaction between the two areas, because each science thinks that this is the business of the other.

EMPIRICAL EVIDENCE

It may be argued that, although there are some spectacular political interventions into the international economy, these are of a transient and more or less random nature and can therefore be safely disregarded compared with long-run market forces. To counter this argument, empirical evidence is adduced by way of example. (Many further empirical studies to the same effect are presented throughout the book.)

INFLUENCE OF POLITICS ON TRADE AND CAPITAL FLOWS

The trade patterns between industrialized countries and less developed countries (LDCs) are strongly influenced by one particular political factor, namely current or former colonial dependence. The hypothesis that 'trade follows the flag' is substantiated by an empirical study (Svedberg 1981) for a whole range of actual and former colonial countries. The evidence here presented is restricted to the two major former colonial powers, the UK and France.

In 1938, at the height of the colonial epoch, 34 per cent of total trade of UK colonies was with the UK, whereas in the case of all LDCs the UK share in total trade amounted to only 19 per cent. This implies a 'colonial ties' ratio (or 'enforcement ratio', as it is sometimes called) of 34:19, or 1.8. This special position of the metropolitan country did not disappear after the colonies were given up; in the case of the United Kingdom it was even strengthened. A quarter of a century later, in 1960–2, the share of the UK in the total trade of her ex-colonies rose slightly, to 37 per cent, while the share of the UK in the total trade of all LDCs dropped to 13 per cent. The 'colonial ties' ratio rose to 37:13, or 2.8. This is shown in table 1.1.

The table shows that the same holds for France, where the 'colonial ties' ratio slightly increased from 7.8 to 7.9. The political (and cultural) influences in the form of colonial ties thus seem to remain in force over a considerable number of years. When the international trade pattern is to be explained, such factors must be taken into account.

TABLE 1.1   The impact of colonial ties on the pattern of trade and foreign direct investment: United Kingdom and France

	1938			1960–62 (trade) 1967 (investment)		
	Metropolitan share	'Colonial ties' ratio		Metropolitan share	'Colonial ties' ratio	
	Own colonies	All LDCs	(unweighted)	Own colonies	All LDCs	(unweighted)
	%	%		%	%	
Trade						
UK	34	19	1.8	37	13	2.8
France	62	8	7.8	63	8	7.9
Foreign direct investment (accumulated stock)						
UK	96	44	2.2	54	19	2.8
France	96	8	12.0	68	9	7.6

Sources: Svedberg (1981), Tables 1, 2 and 5, and own calculations.

The importance of colonial political ties applies not only to trade patterns but also to foreign direct investment. The lower part of table 1.1 shows that the UK and France virtually monopolized investment in 1938: 96 per cent of all foreign-owned stock in their colonies was owned by them. Taking all LDCs, the presence of UK ownership is much smaller (44 per cent) and that of France almost minute (8 per cent). The influence of political factors is most striking especially in the case of France. Though the domination of the metropolitan countries in their own ex-colonies is considerably lower in 1967, it is still much higher than in all LDCs, resulting in a 'colonial ties' ratio of 2.8 for the UK and 7.6 for France.

It is to be concluded that political factors – here, colonial ties – have a strong and persistent effect on the international economy, both on trade and on foreign direct investment. (For further evidence see especially chapters 4 and 8.)

INFLUENCE OF TRADE ON POLITICS

The reverse influence – of the international economy on politics – has also been supported in empirical studies. Thus it has been shown that international trade serves to reduce political conflict. The trade between two nations confers gains to both of them, according to classical trade theory (otherwise they would not engage in it). The loss of existing trade ties arising from a political conflict between two nations implies a welfare loss. The two countries trading with each other therefore make an effort to avoid conflicts in order not to suffer such a welfare loss.

Using multiple regression analysis (in order to control for external factors), this theory has been substantiated for dyadic relationships over 30 countries in the period 1958–67 (Polachek 1980). 'Trade' is measured by exports and imports, and 'conflict' is measured by events data that record hostility reported in 47 newspapers; overall, 126,000 observations were collected. It turns out that there is a strong negative association between trade and conflict: doubling trade between two countries would seem to lead to about a 15–20 per cent decline in the net frequency of hostility between them. (It has been checked that this result refers to the causality running from trade to conflict, and not from conflict to trade.) The study thus suggests that international trade is an important means of furthering the peace between nations.

International trade not only reduces political conflict, but may also intensify the political dependence of a weak country on a strong one. Nations that engage in substantial trade with a dominant partner may be expected to display compliant political behaviour towards it. 'Trade dependence' is operationalized by measuring export dependence and commodity concentration; 'political compliance' is measured by an index of agreement in the UN General Assembly plenary session roll calls, counting the cases in which the small country voted the same way as the dominant one. For the relationship between US voting patterns in the UN and those of its trade-dependent countries, it is shown that such countries are in fact distinctly compliant on Cold War voting issues (Richardson 1976; Richardson and Kegley 1980).

As the analysis presented below (in particular, chapters 5 and

6) shows, there are however definite limits on how far a dominant country may force another country to behave in a desired way. What matters is not that there is a one-way 'power' relationship from big to small, or from rich to poor nations, but rather that there is an *interdependence* in both the economic and the political spheres. It is exactly this interaction that makes it necessary to integrate economics and politics, and to take into account how decision-makers influencing the international political economy behave. To leave out the behaviour of political decision-makers such as governments, interest groups and international organizations, as is usual in traditional international trade theory, is to present a distorted view, because an important part of the politico-economic interaction is thereby left out of account.

Having established that there are good grounds for accepting a strong interaction of economics and politics in the international sphere, and having noted that the fields of international economics and international politics have been separated up to now, the question arises of how this gap can be bridged.

PUBLIC CHOICE

The economic theory of politics, often called public choice, may be used to integrate economic and political studies of international relationships.

The 'public choice' approach seeks to analyse political processes, and the interaction between the economy and the polity, by using the tools of modern (neoclassical) analysis. It provides an explicit study of the workings of political institutions and the behaviour of governments, parties, voters, interest groups and (public) bureaucracies. Public choice is part of an endeavour to apply the 'rational behaviour' approach to areas beyond (traditional) economics (see Becker 1976). In recent years an increasing number of political scientists, sociologists and social psychologists have taken up this approach. It constitutes one of the rare successful examples of interdisciplinary research.

The 'rational behaviour' approach to social problems and 'public choice' theory are characterized by two main features.

Most basically, the individual is taken as the unit of analysis. He is assumed to be 'rational' in the limited sense of responding in a systematic and hence predictable way to incentives; he chooses courses of action that yield the highest net benefits according to his own evaluation (utility function). Contrary to what is often believed by non-economists it is not assumed that individuals are fully informed. Rather, the amount of information they seek is the result of an (often implicit) cost–benefit calculus; indeed, it is shown that in the political arena it often does not pay them to be well informed ('rational ignorance').

The second characteristic of the public choice approach is that an individual's behaviour is explained by concentrating on changes in the *constraints* to which he is exposed. Changes in behaviour are not attributed to (unexplained) shifts in preferences. Individuals are assumed to be capable of comparing alternatives, seeing substitution possibilities and making marginal adjustments.

Public choice is based on the now 'classical' contributions by writers such as Kenneth Arrow, Anthony Downs, James Buchanan, Gordon Tullock, Mancur Olson and William Niskanen, with Joseph Schumpeter as an important forerunner. Current research results are published in leading economic and political science journals. In recent years empirical research in particular has flourished. Applications of public choice cover almost all areas in economics (for surveys see, e.g., Frey 1978, Mueller 1979, Bowls and Whynes 1981), but up to now the international economy has been almost totally neglected.

Public choice has made valuable contributions to economics and political science and should therefore be of interest to all social scientists who want to bridge the gap between economics and international (political) relations. Its contribution when applied to international problems may be seen to go in five directions.

1 The public choice view provides fresh insights into the subject, in the same way that the economics-based approach illuminates general politics. This does not, of course, mean that the approach is superior to any other, but rather that it is able to illuminate particular aspects of international political economics.

2 An advantage of the economic approach to international

political economics is that its analysis is based on an explicit and unified theory of human behaviour, and on a technical apparatus, capable of producing theoretical solutions and empirically testable propositions.

3   The economic approach concentrates on specific aspects of international political economics, making it possible to isolate and analyse relatively simple relationships. This high degree of abstraction helps us to gain insights into complex problem areas.

4   The emphasis on deriving propositions that are, at least in principle, amenable to empirical testing is healthy because it forces the researcher to be realistic. The econometric or politico-metric analyses also provide important factual knowledge about the relationships between the variables studied.

5   The public choice view is interdisciplinary in a specific sense of the word: it combines the economic and political aspects of international political economy but uses only one theoretical approach. (Usually, 'interdisciplinarity' is understood to mean that theoretical approaches must be combined.) This has the advantage that the two areas can be closely united.

So far, the public choice approach has been applied very little to international economics. Some forerunners have made noteworthy contributions. The most important is Albert Hirschman with his *National Power and the Structure of Foreign Trade* (1945). The link established by Hirschman between economics and politics in the international sphere focuses primarily on the classical concept of 'gains from trade'. While all the countries engaged in trade benefit, under a large number of constellations the gains are asymmetrical. An example is provided by a small poor country that carries on a large portion of its trade (say 80 per cent of its exports) with a large wealthy country (for which these transactions account for, say, only 5 per cent of its exports). The small country may then be taken to be more dependent on the larger country than the reverse. Hirschman discusses many such asymmetries and their consequences in his work. Another forerunner is Charles Kindleberger's *Power and Money* (1970). Its subtitle, *The Economics of International Politics and the Politics of International Economics* indicates the wide range of issues treated, including trade wars.

POLITICAL SCIENTISTS' INTERNATIONAL POLITICAL ECONOMY

Within international relations there is also an endeavour to integrate political and economic aspects in the international sphere. This political science approach, called 'international political economy', has recently been surveyed (Barry Jones 1983), and there exist useful collections of articles (Bergsten and Krause 1975, Kegley and McGowan 1981). The most often cited contribution in this field is Robert Keohane and Joseph Nye's *Power and Interdependence* (1977); other basic contributions are by Susan Strange (1971) and Fred Bergsten (1975) on the politics and economics of international currencies, Joan Spero's *Politics of International Economic Relations* (1977), Stephen Krasner's *Defending the National Interest* (1978) and Peter Katzenstein's *Between Power and Plenty* (1978).

Within the political scientist's approach, four major perspectives of international political economy may be distinguished.

1 the mercantilist or neo-mercantilist view, stressing the central role of the nation-state as the sole basic actor, and the only source of security for its citizens;
2 the liberal view, which is associated with neoclassical economics. This economic approach is regarded rather sceptically by proponents of international political economy. For example, one writer argues 'that the corpus of liberal theory rests not upon sound simplifying propositions about reality but upon simplifications which require evasions, or even distortions, of reality if they are to be useable, or a priori assumptions which are quite simply unwarranted' (Barry Jones 1983, p. 175);
3 the radical or Marxist view, which takes the structural inequalities of the international system to be the inevitable product of capitalism. It is taken as a matter of course that the developing countries are exploited by the developed (capitalist) ones;
4 the structuralist perspective (associated with Raul Prebisch), which recognizes the fundamental structural disadvantage of developing countries in relation to industrialized countries but

remains reformist by seeking corrective arrangements through negotiations.

Political scientists do not hesitate to claim international political economy as their proper and exclusive domain. 'Power' and 'authority', and not market relations, are taken to be the central concepts with which to study the problems, and in addition the analysis has to be 'dynamic' and has to take into account historical processes. Accordingly, there is a marked tendency to reject economic theory.

This rejection does not, however, seem to be based on an extensive knowledge of the literature. Hirschman's path-breaking contribution of 1945 is, for example, completely overlooked, and the public choice approach is almost totally disregarded, with the exception of the public goods analysis as developed by Mancur Olson (1965). This neglect is, for instance, evidenced by a political science survey writer proclaiming that 'Neo-classical theory . . . treats political and social processes perfunctorily, as extraneous and at best, exogenous factors' (Tooze 1981, p. 130).

Indeed, the 'classical' writers on public choice (Arrow, Downs, Buchanan, Tullock, Niskanen) are rarely if ever quoted, let alone the specific contributors to this approach mentioned within this book.

From the public choice point of view, political scientists' international political economy is deficient in various respects. The most important shortcoming is its non-analytical structure. It lacks a well-spelled-out theory of behaviour from which to derive (non-obvious) testable hypotheses. Rather, the approach is descriptive, historical and (sometimes) anecdotal. No effort is made to put up clear propositions and to subject them to empirical (econometric) testing. The political scientists' approach is, however, useful in pointing out problems, to giving general insights, and helping to grasp the particular forms of institutions and political processes relevant for international political economics.

PROBLEMS DISCUSSED IN THE BOOK

'International political economics' as presented here focuses on those international problem areas in which the element of political economy is of major importance. These are, at the same time, those areas most grossly neglected by the traditional theory of international trade, which either examines the effects of imposing tariffs and other trade restrictions, or derives an optimal tariff from the point of view of the world or of a single country.

In this book the forces determining the level and structure of tariffs between industries are discussed in chapters 2 and 3. The question of the political factors (in particular, 'country risk') that, together with economic factors, determine the foreign direct investment is taken up in chapter 4. Chapter 5 looks into the question of which countries receive international aid and what they have to do in return for it. Chapter 6 enquires as to whether it is possible to influence other countries to undertake a desired policy by using economic sanctions, i.e. to engage in trade wars. The conditions under which international co-operation comes about, and the specific problems connected with it are the subject of chapter 7. The following chapter deals with the functioning of international organizations. Finally, chapter 9 summarizes the contents and points out the strengths and limits of the approach.

The subjects of multinational corporations, economic imperialism and international cartels are excluded from this study because they are well treated in the existing literature.

APPROACH USED

The standard models of economic theory are applied to the field of international political economics wherever possible. This means, in particular, that the tools of analysis that are employed are well known to students of economics. The economic model of human behaviour, which assumes that individuals aim selfishly at increasing their own utility, is applied throughout. In contrast to traditional economic theory, including trade theory, individuals are assumed to direct their efforts towards furthering their utility not only in the economic (market) sphere, but also in the political process. Great emphasis is put on the insights given by public choice. Thus, it is taken for granted that political decision-makers are endogenous actors within the international politico-economic system. An attempt is made to explain, and not simply describe, the behaviour of voters, governments, public bureaucracies, interest groups and international organizations. 'Countries' or 'nations' do not behave as such; there is no imaginary 'benevolent dictator' who maximizes social welfare; rather, what we observe countries doing is the result of the behaviour of decision-makers acting according to their own advantage. In particular, it will be pointed out repeatedly that the interests of the government (even if democratically elected) do not necessarily coincide with those of the country as a whole. The public choice approach extensively used here is not normative, but tries to explain what *is* (i.e., it is positive). Influencing the international economy is possible only on the basis of a knowledge of the behaviour of the decision-makers involved. As a purely theoretical discussion is often incapable of throwing light fully on the issues involved, an effort is made here to adduce empirical evidence, usually based on econometric techniques.

CONCLUSION

The international economy is heavily political, but the theory of international economics has as a whole refused to take into account the fact that political factors influence the international economy, and that the international economy in turn influences politics. A range of issues is discussed in this book, showing how important it is to combine economics and political factors in order to understand international (economic) issues. For this purpose, standard economic theory is used, but particular emphasis is placed on using the insight offered by public choice.

FURTHER READING

WORKS MENTIONED IN THE TEXT

Barry Jones, R. J. (1983), 'Perspectives on International Political Economy'. In R. J. Barry Jones (ed.), *Perspectives on Political Economy*. London: Pinter, 169–208.
Becker, Gary S. (1976), *The Economic Approach to Human Behavior*. Chicago: University of Chicago Press.

Bergsten, C. Fred (1975), *The Dilemma of the Dollar*. New York: New York University Press.

Bergsten, C. Fred and Krause, Lawrence B. (eds) (1975), *World Politics and International Economics*. Washington, DC: Brookings Institution.

Bowls, Roger and Whynes, David K. (1981), *The Economic Theory of the State*. Oxford: Martin Robertson.

Frey, Bruno S. (1978), *Modern Political Economy*. Oxford: Martin Robertson.

Hirschman, Albert O. (1945), *National Power and the Structure of Foreign Trade*. Berkeley: University of California Press; reprinted 1969.

Katzenstein, Peter J. (ed.) (1978), *Between Power and Plenty: Foreign Economic Policies of Advanced Industrial States*. Madison: University of Wisconsin Press.

Kegley, Charles W. and McGowan, Patrick (eds) (1981), *The Political Economy of Foreign Policy Behavior*. Beverly Hills: Sage.

Keohane, Robert O. and Nye, Joseph (1977), *Power and Interdependence*. Boston: Little, Brown.

Kindleberger, Charles P. (1970), *Power and Money. The Economics of International Politics and the Politics of International Economics*. New York: Basic Books.

Krasner, Stephen (1978), *Defending the National Interests*. Princeton: Princeton University Press.

Mueller, Dennis C. (1979), *Public Choice*. Cambridge: Cambridge University Press.

Olson, Mancur (1965), *The Logic of Collective Action: Public Goods and the Theory of Groups*. Cambridge, Mass.: Harvard University Press.

Polachek, Solomon W. (1980), 'Conflict and Trade'. *Journal of Conflict Resolution*, 24 (March), 55–78.

Richardson, Neil R. (1976), 'Political Compliance and US Trade Dominance'. *American Political Science Review*, 70 (December), 1098–1109.

Richardson, Neil R. and Kegley, Charles W. (1980), 'Trade Dependence and Foreign Policy Compliance: A Longitudinal Analysis'. *International Studies Quarterly*, 24 (June), 191–222.

Spero, Joan E. (1977), *The Politics of International Economic Relations*. London: Allen and Unwin.

Strange, Susan (1971), *Sterling and British Policy. A Political Study of an International Currency in Decline*. London: Oxford University Press.

Svedberg, Peter (1981), 'Colonial Enforcement of Foreign Direct Investment'. *Manchester School of Economic and Social Studies*, 49 (March), 21–38.
Tooze, Roger (1981), 'Economics, International Political Economy and Change in the International System'. In B. Buzan and R. J. Barry Jones (eds), *Change and the Study of International Relations. The Evaded Dimension*. London: Pinter, 120–37.

WORKS RELATING TO FURTHER ASPECTS DISCUSSED

So far, there are only two texts which (partly) cover the topic of this book:

Willett, Thomas D. (1979), 'Some Aspects of the Public Choice Approach to International Economic Relations'. Paper prepared for the European University Institute Conference on 'New Economic Approaches to the Study of International Integration: Applications to Political Decision-making', Florence, May–June 1979; mimeo.
Frey, Bruno S. (1984). 'The Public Choice View of International Political Economy'. *International Organization* 38 (Winter), 199–223.

Besides Hirschmann (1945) and Kindleberger (1970), another early contribution to international political economics is a book in German:

Bernholz, Peter (1966), *Aussenpolitik internationale Wirtschaftsbeziehungen*. Frankfurt: Klostermann.

Very few (and only introductory) textbooks on international economics treat some aspects of international political economics:

Walter, Ingo and Areskoug, Kaj (1981), *International Economics*, 3rd edn. New York: John Wiley.
Kindleberger, Charles P. and Lindert, Peter H. (1978), *International Economics*, 6th edn. Homewood, Ill.: Richard D. Irwin.

Important contributions to political scientists' international political economy not yet mentioned are:

Cohen, Benjamin J. (1977), *Organizing the World's Money: The Political Economy of International Monetary Relations*. London: Macmillan.

Gilpin, Robert (1975), *US Power and the Multinational Corporation. The Political Economy of Foreign Direct Investment*. London: Macmillan.

Knorr, Klaus (1973), *Power and Wealth. The Political Economy of International Power*. London: Macmillan.

2

How do Tariffs Come About?
Theoretical Approach

TARIFF BARGAINING AS THE RULE

In the years 1964–7, the United States and the countries of the European Economic Community embarked on what came to be known as the 'Kennedy Round'. After a slow process of negotiation (in which many other countries also participated) and interminable haggling over reciprocity, an agreement was reached that led to an almost 50 per cent (average) reduction in tariffs.

This is just one example of innumerable international trade negotiations that are all characterized by hard bargaining: a country (or group of countries) is prepared to reduce its import tariffs only if the other country (or group of countries) is prepared to reciprocate. Tariff reductions are thus typically arrived at by mutual concessions of the participating countries.

OPTIMALITY OF FREE TRADE

This bargaining must come as a surprise to a student of the theory of international trade. This theory makes two general propositions of fundamental importance.

1   World welfare is maximized by free trade.
2   A country's welfare is maximized by a unilateral shift to free trade.

The second proposition suggests that no bargaining or reciprocity between countries is necessary in order to increase welfare: it is in every country's own interest to abolish tariffs, even if the other countries do not follow. This proposition is usually illustrated by figure 2.1, which for simplicity considers only two commodities, X_1 and X_2. The production possibility frontier FF gives the maximum quantities of the goods X_1 and X_2 that can be produced with given resources. Welfare is presented by the community indifference curves I. The highest welfare level possible without international trade (I_1) is reached at point A, where the slopes of the production possibility curve and the indifference curve are the same: the marginal rate of transformation is equal to the marginal rate of substitution and is equal to the relative price at which the goods exchange (given by the slope of the internal relative price line, pp).

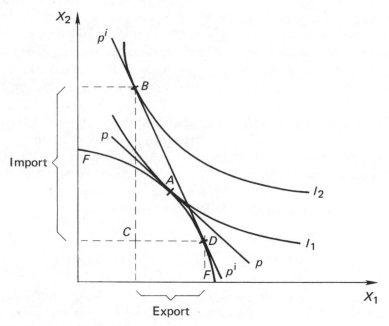

FIGURE 2.1 The gains from trade.

If the international price line p^ip^i is different from the internal price pp, it pays the country to reallocate its production and to profit from international trade. Employing the international exchange or price ratio p^ip^i, the country can now reach the higher indifference curve I_2 at point B. The country exports DC of good X_1, and imports CB of good X_2. The marginal rates of transformation and substitution are still equal, thus ensuring Pareto optimality. Any measure that prevents the achievement of these marginal equality rules lowers potential economic welfare. The most important intervention is tariffs, which lead to a deviation of the prices paid by consumers from the prices paid in the rest of the world. Consumers shift along their indifference curve until the marginal rate of substitution in consumption equals the relative price between the goods within the country, but this will no longer equal the marginal rate of transformation in production in the rest of the world. This means that the imposition of tariffs reduces the amount of welfare that is achievable.

The size of the welfare loss arising from the imposition of tariffs has been empirically measured. For this purpose, figure 2.2,

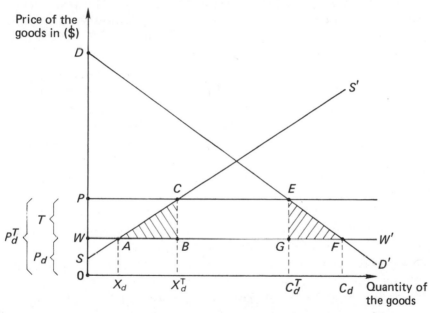

FIGURE 2.2 Measurement of the welfare loss arising from a tariff.

showing the demand and supply for a particular product, is used. DD' represents the demand curve and SS' the supply curve, for the good produced by an industry. Given the exchange rate and the world price of the industry's good, the industry faces the perfectly elastic world supply curve at the domestic price P_d. When there is free trade, domestic consumption is OC_d, production is OX_d and imports are X_dC_d. The area below the demand curve DD' (which shows the marginal utility of the consumption of the good) gives total consumer welfare, $ODFC_d$, from which the cost of buying the good ($P_d \cdot OC_d$) has to be deducted. Consumer surplus thus equals WDF. The imposition of a tariff of T monetary units (dollars) per unit of the good ($T = t \cdot P_d$, with t the ad valorem tariff rate) results in a domestic price of P_d^T. Domestic consumption is reduced to OC_d^T, production is increased to OX_d^T, and imports are reduced to $X_d^TC_d^T$. When tariff T is imposed consumer surplus falls from WDF (in free trade) to PDE. The loss is $WPEF$. However, not all of this represents social costs: tariff revenues (which are $BCEG$) and producer surplus (which increases by $WPCA$) represent *transfers* of income within the members of the country considered. The *true social cost* of protection by the tariff equals the so-called dead-weight loss triangles ACB and GEF (indicated by the shaded areas in the figure).

The empirical estimates of the social cost of protection have, with few exceptions, arrived at low values compared with gross national product (GNP). Table 2.1 gives some representative examples of the welfare gain that could be achieved if tariffs were reduced. It may be seen that, in the case of both unilateral and multilateral tariff reductions, the estimated welfare gains are rather small, typically below 1 per cent of GNP. This estimation procedure has, however, recently been challenged, because of the neglect of the temporal effects. The main benefits of a tariff reduction occur over time. It is therefore necessary to calculate the present value of these future benefits. Robert Baldwin and his co-workers (1980) found that the net benefit of a 50 per cent multilateral tariff reduction was large, amounting to over $1 billion (at the 1976 value). The cost to labour and capital brought about by the necessary adjustments were fully taken into account.

Easton and Grubel (1983) argue that the discount rate used is mistaken: the benefits of tariff reductions should be taken to increase at the rate at which international trade can be expected to grow in the future, not only because of GNP growth but also as a result of reduced transport costs and economies of scale of internationally traded goods, while the benefits of tariffs grow only at the pace of GNP growth. It follows that the benefits of

TABLE 2.1 Empirical estimates of the welfare gain from unilateral and bilateral tariff reductions: results from static and dynamic studies

Country	Size of welfare gain (absolute or as percentage of GNP)	Author
Static studies		
UK (elimination of tariffs with European Economic Community)	At most 1%	Johnson (1958)
United States (elimination of import tariffs)	0.5–0.7%	Magee (1972)
Kennedy Round	Less than	Balassa and Kreinin (1967)
Tokyo Round	0.25%	Brown and Whalley (1980)
Dynamic studies		
United States (multilateral tariff reduction by 50%)	over $1 billion (at the 1976 value)	Baldwin, Mutti and Richardson (1980)
(unilateral and multilateral tariff reductions)	Very large	Easton and Grubel (1983)

*The studies are cited in the references given at the end of the chapter.

freer trade are an increasing function of time and therefore can become very high, both absolutely and in relation to GNP. The dynamic analyses thus suggest that unilateral or multilateral reductions or eliminations of tariffs yield sizeable welfare gains to the population of a country.

In international trade theory it is pointed out that interventions in foreign trade may be used in order to achieve nationwide goals, such as the support of infant industries, self-sufficiency, military preparedness or in a trade war (see discussion in chapter 6).

According to Johnson (1969, p. 186), 'the only valid argument for protection as a means of maximizing economic welfare is the optimum tariff argument', all the other 'national' goals being better attainable by measures other than trade restriction. The optimum tariff argument states that under certain conditions a country may improve its material well-being by imposing restrictions on its exports or imports, if this leads to a reduction in the (pre-tariff) prices of imports and/or to a rise in the (world market) prices of its exports. The corresponding welfare gains, however, can be achieved only at the expense of the economic welfare of the trading partners. The imposition of such (from the point of view of a particular country) 'optimal' tariffs is likely to lead to retaliations, so that the outcome may well be a general increase of tariffs and a general decline of welfare.

RECONCILIATION OF THEORY AND REALITY

Economic theory convincingly argues that free trade leads to the most efficient allocation of resources and maximizes a country's economic welfare. Empirical research shows that unilateral and bilateral tariff reductions yield significant welfare gains. Reality teaches us, however, that tariffs (and other trade restrictions) are prevalent in all periods and countries, and that there is a continuous danger of ever-increasing protectionism in the world. The attempts made to reduce protectionism are based on the notion of reciprocity; i.e., the propositions of trade theory about the welfare-increasing results of free trade do not seem to be accepted.

The glaring gap between theory and reality could be attributed to two causes. First, it might be argued that the policy-makers are misinformed and/or of limited intelligence and therefore do not realize the welfare-increasing effect of unilateral tariff reductions. It may well be that producers and workers in some export sectors do not fully comprehend that higher import tariffs may threaten export sales because the costs of imports will rise, other nations will retaliate or foreign income will fall. The same may sometimes apply to consumers who are not fully aware that import barriers increase their cost of living. However, misperception and lack of intelligence can explain only a (small) part of the protectionist activity; detailed studies of debates over trade legislation reveal a rather remarkable degree of knowledge on the part of the groups affected.

The second explanation is more relevant. It notes that the assumptions underlying the pure theory of international trade do not fully pertain in reality. In particular, it may not be assumed that markets are perfect: real economies are subject to imperfect competition, distorting relative prices; and there are non-negligible costs of information, transactions and bargaining. Markets are thus not perfectly flexible, and it proves difficult and sometimes impossible to undertake the redistributions necessary to compensate the losers from a (potentially) Pareto-optimal trade-liberalizing measure.

Once the world of perfectly competitive and frictionless exchange is left behind, political forces must be taken into account. This has been neglected in the established international trade theory. The traditional approach assumes away the question of how the free trade optimum can be attained. Instead, it postulates the existence of a benign, omniscient government that can use non-distortionary taxes and subsidies to place society at a point on the utility possibility frontier. If these assumptions are found not to hold in reality, a protectionist stand can be interpreted as a rational policy for decision-makers in a democracy.

PROTECTIONIST PRESSURES IN A DEMOCRACY

In a democracy, the will of the majority should decide. As a (unilateral) shift to free trade increases welfare, according to economic theory, it could be expected that the government would win votes by abolishing tariffs. By definition of Pareto optimality, either a majority of the electorate benefits directly, or the gains accruing to a minority can be redistributed so that a majority of the electorate is better off. In a system of direct simple majority rule in an assembly, the *median voter* (the one who makes a majority out of a minority) would cast his vote in favour of free trade. The median voter model, however, is based on a set of assumptions that in important respects do not represent reality.

Their modification provides an explanation for the existence, and possibly growth, of tariffs in a democracy. There are five important modifications and extensions to consider (Baldwin 1976).

1   The losers of a tariff reduction – the people engaged in the domestic production of the goods concerned – are not necessarily compensated. If they form a stable majority, they will obstruct the reduction and/or elimination of tariffs. The median voter model would then predict that protectionism prevails.

2   The prospective gainers have less incentive to participate in the vote, to inform themselves and to organize and support a pressure group than do the losers. Tariff reductions are a public good whose benefits are received by everybody, including those not taking the trouble or incurring the cost to bring about the reduction. The benefits for the gainers of a tariff reduction are, moreover, uncertain and take place in the future, and are therefore less visible. The losers of a tariff reduction, on the other hand, experience their loss much more directly, and will therefore engage more intensively in the political process.

3   There is a possibility that the prospective losers from free trade may be better represented in parliament and in the government than the prospective winners. This is the case, for instance, when the prospective losers are favourably distributed regionally. If they have a 51 per cent majority in two out of three voting districts, they need only 34 per cent of the total vote to gain a majority in parliament. If they have a 51 per cent majority in 13 out of 25 voting districts, the group dominates parliament on the basis of a vote share of 27 per cent.

4   Log rolling, or vote-trading, can strongly affect the outcome of majority voting. Vote-trading may happen if groups of voters have unequal preference intensities for two issues. This is very likely to be the case where tariffs are concerned. Consider a group I of voters engaged in domestic, import-competing activities. Their main preference is against the reduction of tariffs for their *own* products (proposition A) and weakly in favour of the

reduction of tariffs for some other products (proposition B). Assume another group of voters, group II, whose main interest lies in maintaining the tariff for the products concerned in B, and who have a weak preference for tariff reduction in A. If neither of the two groups has a majority, and the other voters perceive the benefits of free trade, both propositions A and B would be accepted and free trade established. If, however, groups I and II combined have a majority, they can agree to trade votes: group I votes against the tariff reduction that group II strongly opposes (i.e against proposition B), provided that group II votes against the tariff reduction that group I strongly opposes (i.e. against proposition A). This then leads to a majority vote against tariff reductions; propositions A and B are both defeated.

5 Tariffs provide revenue for governments, which in their absence would find it more difficult to finance public expenditure. This is especially true in developing countries, where, owing to the inefficiency of the tax system, there is little tax revenue. Table 2.2 shows that in many less developed countries tariff revenues constitute a dominant part of total tax revenues. In Gambia the share was 66 per cent; in Yemen, Swaziland, Rwanda and Zaïre the tariff revenues still accounted for more than half of total

TABLE 2.2   Taxes on international transactions as a proportion of central government revenue, selected developing countries, 1972–7*

	%
Gambia	66
Yemen	63
Swaziland	54
Rwanda	52
Zaïre	52
Bahamas	49
Chad	48
Ecuador	47

*The average figures may for some countries relate to less than six years.
Source: David Greenaway, 'Taxes on International Transactions and Economic Development'. In Alan T. Peacock and Francesco Forte (eds), *The Political Economy of Taxation*. Oxford: Basil Blackwell, 1981, 131–47.

revenues. A government in such a country would have a great interest in securing this income source, and for this reason would oppose free trade.

These five modifications of the simple median voter model combine to explain why free trade, which is optimal from the point of view of the country as a whole, is not actually found in reality. The discussion suggests that, on the contrary, there is a *political market for protection*. Protection is demanded by particular groups of voters, firms and associated interest groups and parties, and is supplied by politicians and civil servants. Economic interests seek to gain advantages and to improve their position by turning to the political system. They invest resources (labour and finance) in order to influence political decisions in their favour. Such activities, which are in general unproductive because they do not – at least not directly – increase the value of goods and services available, are a special form of profit maximization. Such profits can be gained by lobbying for trade barriers (tariffs, quotas), which generate rents which the particular actors can acquire for themselves (rent-seeking); or they can be gained by competing in the political process in order to appropriate the monetary revenues from tariffs (revenue-seeking).

The political market for protection will now be discussed in some detail, concentrating first on the demand for, and then on the supply of, protection.

DEMAND FOR PROTECTION

Organized economic groups that seek to gain protection from international competition by raising the tariff level may be assumed to compare the cost and benefits of such activity (Baldwin 1982). In figure 2.3 the horizontal axis measures the increase in the tariff level attained; the origin thus indicates the tariff level existing at the outset. The vertical axis measures the cost and the benefit from such action in comparable monetary units. *OA* is the 'cost-of-lobbying' curve, showing the total cost in

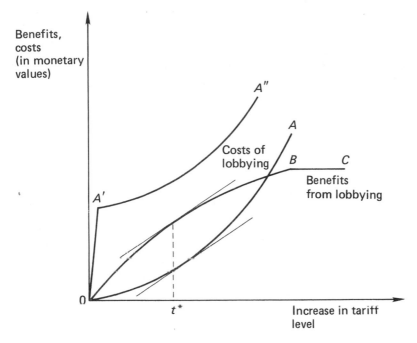

FIGURE 2.3 The optimal amount of lobbying for tariff protection.

monetary terms of securing tariff protection by lobbying, given the organizational structures of the respective group. This curve has a rising slope because it is reasonable to assume that it becomes increasingly difficult for a particular economic interest group to raise the tariff in its favour; in other words, there are rising marginal costs. The cost-of-lobbying curve reflects the willingness of political suppliers to grant additional protection to that particular economic interest (sector or industry). The cost curve will be the lower (1) the better the economic interest is organized, (2) the more efficiently the lobbying activity is undertaken, and (3) the more the other groups in society feel that this particular economic interest should receive tariff protection. An example are the farmers, whose protection against foreign competition is rather altruistically favoured for traditional reasons by many people in society. A less altruistic reason for favouring a tariff increase may be that interest groups other than the one concerned think that such action will increase their own chances of receiving tariff protection in the future; in effect, they endeavour to bring about a type of political exchange.

Returning to figure 2.3, *OBC* shows the 'benefits-from-protection' curve. This indicates the monetary value of tariff protection from the point of view of the group undertaking the lobbying activity. The larger the increase in the tariff, the higher the benefits accruing to the group, up to *B*, which marks the maximum protection implied by the prohibitive tariff. The benefit curve's slope is not determined *a priori*; it is not inconceivable that increasing tariffs yield increasing marginal benefits, at least over a limited range. The curve shown in figure 2.3 depicts decreasing marginal benefits over the whole range. The group's lobbying effort is optimal when it leads to an associated tariff increase t^*, at which point the 'rent', in the form of the difference between benefits and cost, is maximized. The figure is able to illustrate that a lobbying activity to increase tariff protection need not necessarily be worthwhile for a particular economic interest group. There may be such high initial costs of lobbying (given by OA'), that the cost curve $OA'A''$ lies above the benefit-from-lobbying curve OBC over the whole range. In this case there is no positive rent from lobbying.

This cost constellation may occur when the economic interests are difficult to organize, for example if there are high set-up costs to engaging in political lobbying. Figure 2.3 stresses the importance of having an established organization to further one's interests in the political market (or in any such market) for protection. If the cost of initial organization were already covered (for instance, because the organization already exists for other purposes such as social gatherings), it would be advantageous to embark on lobbying. In that case, the cost-of-lobbying curve is OA, and the associated optimal tax increase is t^*. This explains why economic interests that are already organized have a tendency to get additional advantages, thereby, establishing their privileged position even more strongly, while newcomers find it difficult to make their demands felt in the political struggle.

While the model is instructive, in reality the extent of lobbying and protection achieved can be explained only if the factors determining the position and slope of the cost and benefit curves can be empirically measured. This has indeed been done, by comparing the conditions existing in various sectors or industries. We now turn to these aspects.

PRO-TARIFF GROUPS

The *domestic firms in competition* with foreign firms supplying in the home market have the strongest interest in tariff protection, and generally oppose free trade policies. They are joined by the workers and trade unions of that economic sector, who know that they can share the rents achieved by tariff protection. Firms producing complementary products and supplying inputs to the import-competing firms are another group favouring protection (provided they do not themselves strongly depend on imported raw materials).

The protectionist groups usually have strong political interests, because the effects of a change in protection are visible and direct, and therefore carry a lot of weight in the political debate. These groups can easily argue that a tariff reduction would result in a direct loss to them, reducing output and employment, while favouring foreign interests. Increased protection, on the other hand (so they will claim), would obviously increase the employment of nationals and the output and profits of domestic producers. These arguments are particularly forceful, and are actively promoted by trade unions, when there is an abnormally high level of unemployment in the domestic economy.

ANTI-TARIFF GROUPS

The main group in society favouring trade-liberalizing policies and opposing protection are the export suppliers. Firms offering their products on foreign markets realize that increased protectionism at home may lead to retaliation by foreign countries, threatening their sales. They cannot expect to widen their access to foreign markets if their own country is not prepared to reduce its protection. It is, however, quite difficult to translate these export interests into effective political action. The damage suffered through import restrictions is indirect; it has the character of a foregone opportunity which is difficult to quantify.

Among the firms opposing tariffs are the *multinationals*. They tend to favour free trade because they are able to compete efficiently on international markets. Also, protectionist tendencies may lead to restrictions in their own activities, in the extreme leading to the nationalization of their property in the foreign country retaliating to protectionist actions in the home country.

Domestic firms using imported inputs for their production comprise another group interested in trade liberalization. Such firms, however, often belong at the same time to the import-competing sector which has an interest in protection, so that their political position becomes equivocal or even pro-tariff.

Consumers and their organizations (as far as they exist) also have an interest in low tariffs. Trade barriers burden consumers, who find they have a smaller choice of products and have to pay higher prices for what is available. Consumer groups, however, have little effect on trade policy. One reason is that consumers are normally also employees and workers. Their income is usually exclusively from this source while expenditures are distributed over many different goods, some of which are not (directly) affected by tariffs. As a consequence, it is individually rational for consumers to pay most attention to their position on the producer side, which often benefits from import protection. Another reason why consumers have little impact on trade policy is that the loss of consumer welfare through the imposition of tariffs is rather difficult to identify. It is hard to determine what the prices of the various products would be if tariffs were reduced or abolished, particularly when there is inflation, which easily overwhelms the small income effects. The 'invisibility' and indirectness of the opportunity cost of tariffs hardly motivates consumers to fight politically for tariff reductions. This lack of engagement only partially compensates the importers and distributors of foreign-produced consumption goods (such as retail chains, mail-order houses and discount firms) which have an obvious interest in a lessening of trade restrictions.

POLITICAL ORGANIZATION

Whether the pro-tariff or the anti-tariff interests prevail in a country depends on the political weight of the corresponding groups, and the intensity with which they raise their demands in the political process. A crucial factor is the ability and incentive to organize and to obtain the financing necessary for effective lobbying. As has been pointed out, protection constitutes a public good affecting all the members of a particular economic sector or occupation. There is an incentive for people not to join the interest group or to contribute financially, because they may profit from the outcome in any case. Even if in an industry the benefit from further protection may be very large, it may be difficult or even impossible to raise the lobbying funds because of this tendency towards 'free-riding'. The same problem holds even more strongly for anti-tariff interests, as it is possible to benefit from lower prices and improved export chances without having joined the respective interest group.

There are three conditions under which interest groups are likely to form in the presence of public goods:

1 when the group has been formed for some reason other than a lobby, or has been established by government decree (as, in some countries, with farmers' organizations);
2 when group members get specific private goods, such as information or insurance, only from belonging to the organization;
3 when there is a small-group situation in which the members can impose sanctions on would-be free-riders.

It can be said quite generally that these conditions are more likely to obtain on the producer than on the consumer side. In a given sector, there are often few producers who find it easy to organize. Since, according to our discussion, the import-competing and associated producers have on balance more to gain than the other producers from protection from trade liberalization, this means that pro-tariff lobbying will be stronger. The opposite holds for the consumers interested in free trade. Because of their large numbers and diffuse interests, they are difficult to organize in an effective way, and it is almost impossible to raise funds for such general consumer interests as low tariffs. Consequently, anti-tariff lobbying is comparatively weak.

We therefore have two general propositions concerning the demands for protection.

1 Pro-tariff interests have strong lobbies and consist mainly of import-competing producers (which includes the workers).
2 Anti-tariff interests have weak lobbies, as consumers and exporters find it difficult, and have little incentive, to organize and to lobby effectively.

Note that the interests organize along *industry* or *sector* lines, and not along factor lines, as suggested by the Stolper–Samuelson (1941) approach (or much earlier, of course, by the Marxist theory of the struggle between capital and labour). That traditional theory of trade suggested that all capital interests would promote free trade (if that factor were internationally more competitive) and all labour interests would seek protection, or vice versa if labour were internationally more competitive. It was not expected that part of labour would be for protection and the other part for free trade, and that capital interests would be similarly divided on the free trade issue. In contrast to the traditional Stolper–Samuelson view, the politico-economic approach emphasizes the *rents* that the factors of production acquire through protection from foreign competition. In an industry that therewith gains monopoly profits, the trade unions will attempt to get a share of these rents. As a result, the industry will be characterized by high wages, and by barriers to entry in the factor market of this industry. Factor mobility will be curtailed by the actions of the interest groups, so that one of the basic assumptions of the traditional model of international trade will no longer obtain. *Both* factors of production have an interest in defending the rent they share among themselves, and they will therefore act in concert.

The two contrasting theories of international trade lobbying along factor and industry divisions have been subjected to an empirical analysis (Magee 1980). Twenty-one industries were counted to have engaged in lobbying about the American President's trade bill in 1973. For each such industry the position of labour and capital (represented by the managers) has also been identified. This allows the construction of a 2 × 2 table in which the 21 industries are classified according to whether labour was protectionist or free trade. The result is shown in table 2.3.

TABLE 2.3   A Classification of 21 US industries according to their protectionist or free trade position on the president's trade bill, 1973

Position of capital	Position of labour	
	Protectionist	Free trade
Protectionist	Distilling Textiles Apparel Chemicals Plastics Rubber shoes Leather Shoes Stone, etc. Iron/steel Cutlery Hardware Bearings Watches	Tobacco
Free trade	Petroleum	Paper Machinery Tractors Trucks Aviation

Source: Magee (1980)

If lobbying takes place along the industry lines, all the observations would be in the upper left – lower right diagonal cells in the table; if it takes place along the factor lines, all the observations would be in one of the other cells. According to the table, 19 of the 21 industries fall along this diagonal. Labour and capital almost always take the same position towards the protectionist/free trade issue. Only in the case of the tabacco and the petroleum industry do they not fight on the same front. This analysis strongly supports the politico-economic notion that it is *industries* that are the relevant units of organization on international trade issues.

SUPPLY OF PROTECTION

Tariff levels and changes are determined by political decisions in which the politicians (in particular, the government) and the civil servants (or bureaucracy) are dominant. Trade policy is not decided by direct referendum (not even in Switzerland); voters do not have the chance to vote for or against a particular tariff rate. Protection versus free trade is only one of the issues over which an election is fought, and in most countries and time periods trade policy is dominated by internal economic and political issues.

The government may be assumed to pursue certain ideological goals, but it is subject to a variety of constraints. Among its ideological goals may be its position with respect to protection. A government composed of, or dominated by, a liberal party may, *ceteris paribus*, be expected to open up trade. The most important constraint a government has to observe is the need to be re-elected. If it fears it will lose a forthcoming election, it will undertake a policy that promises to raise its popularity with the voters. A party ideologically committed to free trade may be forced to resort to protectionism if it thinks that such a policy will improve its re-election chances. We have seen that, in the case of foreign trade, the consumer-voters interested in free trade are not very committed, while the interest groups demanding protection try to exert as much influence as possible by lobbying. A government uncertain of re-election will therefore turn its attention to the demands for protection raised by the organized interest groups, hoping that they will deliver some votes and/or provide help in financing the election campaign.

The government has to act within the constraints set by the budget and the balance of payments. The extent to which the constraints restrict the government depends on the structure of the economy and the prevailing economic conditions. The government of a country that runs a high balance of payments deficit may have to resort to protectionist measures in order to indicate to the population its willingness to do something about it, even if the politicians in charge are ideologically opposed to raising tariffs (or find this measure not very effective in curing a deficit in the balance of payments).

Another actor playing an important role in tariff formation is the *public administration*. This body has considerable influence on the 'supply side' of the tariff because it prepares, formulates and implements trade bills. The activity of civil servants with respect to tariffs may again be analysed with the help of the 'rational' model of behaviour, for example by assuming that they will seek to maximize their utility subject to constraints set from outside. The main elements in the civil servants' utility function may be assumed to be the prestige, power and influence that they enjoy relative to the group of people they are officially designed to 'serve' – their clientele. In most cases this clientele will be located in a specific economic sector. For example, in the case of public officials in the ministry of agriculture, the clientele would be those groups with agricultural interests. Public officials are, moreover, proud of being able to show that they are competent in their job ('performance excellence'). They will therefore tend to fight for the interests of 'their' economic sector, and will work for tariffs and other import restrictions in order to protect it from outside competition. They will prefer to use instruments under their own control than to follow general rules imposed by formal laws, and will thus prefer various kinds of non-tariff protection and support (subsidies) to general tariffs.

The political constraints faced by the civil service are imposed by parliament and government. However, both of these actors have little incentive to control public administration tightly, because they are dependent on it in order to reach their own goals. In addition, the political actors have less information available to them than the civil service, in particular with respect to the sometimes very complex issues of protection. The limited incentive of politicians to control the public administration gives civil servants considerable discretionary power; which they can use to their own advantage in the area of trade policy.

The idea that public officials pursue the common interest or collective welfare and therefore fight for free trade has to be rejected. Indeed, it may be argued that they favour greater protection than do politicians. As many civil service departments are organized along industry lines, they depend more strongly on the relationship with this particular industry than do the politicians. Moreover, the civil service has a more limited set of instruments available than the government, which has control over the whole range of economic policy. As a consequence, the individual departments must reach their goals by using the instruments at hand *more intensively*: they will strive to protect the economic sector they are associated with against foreign competition more strongly than will the government politicians, which have other means available to support the respective industry if it is in their interest to do so (Messerlin 1981).

The role of the civil service in the protection against foreign competition has been specifically analysed for the United States (Finger et al. 1982). Trade restrictions are seldom voted on directly by Congress; the commonly used instrument for international protection is the administrative regulation of imports. Under the so-called 'escape clause', an industry that feels 'injured' from imports may petition the International Trade Commission (ITC) to conduct an investigation about this claim. The report by the ITC goes to the President, who then makes a decision on whether and how to prevent or remedy the injury.

Even more important are the 'less-than-fair-value cases' concerned with the sale of subsidized exports in the US market, and anti-dumping cases with sales in the United States at a price below the foreign producer's long-run costs, or below his home market price. The decision of whether these charges are accepted is taken on a 'technical' level by the administration (Treasury Department). This is a possible avenue for domestic producers seeking to gain protection against foreign competition; the domestic users and consumers of imported goods are not directly involved, and have little to say because the procedures are technical and therefore amenable only to the highly trained experts of the interest groups of domestic producers and the civil service. The absence of advocates of free trade allows the public administration and government to serve the domestic producers without being called to task by the disadvantaged buyers of foreign imports, particularly the consumers.

POLITICAL EQUILIBRIUM

Tariffs are the outcome of an interplay between the demand and supply sides of the political market for protection. A simple model has been constructed (Findlay and Wellisz 1983) which shows how a pro-tariff and an anti-tariff interest group fight to get their way, and how the outcome of this struggle leads to an endogenously determined tariff level.

Following traditional trade theory only two goods are considered: the agricultural good, produced with the factor land, and the manufacturing good, produced with the factor capital. Labour is used in both sectors and is taken from a common pool $\bar{L}$. Competition is assumed to be perfect. The economy is taken to have a relative advantage in manufactured goods, which it exports; agricultural goods are imported. As was argued above, the manufacturers will lobby for low tariffs since this increases their export chances; the farm interests will lobby for higher tariffs because this protects them from foreign competition. The manufacturing interests spend labour L_M in order to promote free trade, while farming interests use labour L_F in an attempt to increase tariffs T. The 'tariff lobby function' is

$$T = f(L_M, L_F) \text{ with } \frac{\partial f}{\partial L_M} < 0, \frac{\partial f}{\partial L_F} > 0. \tag{2.1}$$

In order to concentrate on the outcome of the struggle between the farmers' pro-tariff and the manufacturers' anti-tariff lobbying, the political system is assumed to be strongly competitive, so that the government and the civil service are forced to yield to the outcome of the lobbying struggle between the two interest groups.

The fight over tariff-setting is described by a so-called Cournot–Nash process, in which each group takes the lobbying effort of the other group as given, and then calculates its own optimal input of lobbying resources on this basis. The reaction function of the manufacturers is indicated by MM' in figure 2.4; the reaction function of the farmers by FF'. Assume, for example, that farmers employ L_F^0 lobbying resources in order to push up the tariff. The manufacturers respond by choosing point P_0 on their reaction curve MM' and employ L_M^0 lobbying resources. This prompts the farmers to choose P_1 on their reaction curve FF' and to increase their lobbying effort to L_F^1. This induces manufacturers to increase their effort to L_M^1; etc. The reaction curves of the pro- and anti-tariff groups as drawn in

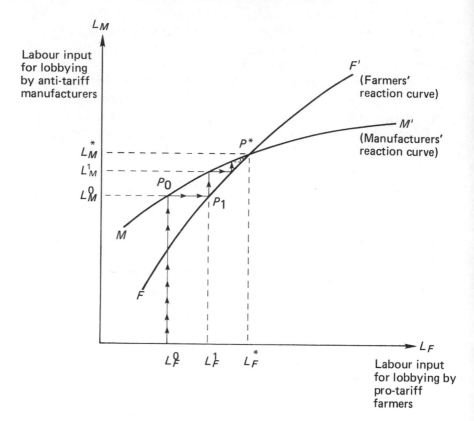

FIGURE 2.4 The struggle of a pro-tariff (farmers') and an anti-tariff (manufacturers') interest group: reaction curves and equilibrium.

the figure lead to a stable equilibrium at P^*. This is the only point at which the lobbying efforts of the two interest groups are consistent with each other: neither is induced to change its lobbying outlays. The manufacturers spend L_M^*, the farmers L_F^*. The equilibrium determines the total level $(L_M^* + L_F^*)$ and distribution (L_F^*/L_M^*) of lobbying expenditures, as well as the level of the tariff T^* (by equation 2.1).

As is shown in figure 2.5, an equilibrium above and to the left of P^* is associated with a lower tariff (say T'), because, given L_F^*, the anti-tariff manufacturers use more resources L'_M to influence the tariff in a downward direction. Accordingly, an equilibrium below P^* (say P^{**}) is associated with a higher tariff (say T'')

because the anti-tariff manufacturers spend relatively less on lobbying compared with the pro-tariff farmers.

The model specifies in simple terms a general equilibrium which determines what part of total resources $\bar{L}$ is used to produce economic goods (in agriculture and manufacturing) and what part is used for rent-seeking. The labour force in economically productive use is $L^* = \bar{L} - (L_M^* + L_F^*)$, and the welfare loss owing to political strife is $w(L_M^* + L_F^*)$, where w is the economic value of labour. The model analyses the protectionist struggle from a highly aggregated point of view. Its main weakness is that the public goods character of tariffs and free trade and the concomitant free-rider effects are not taken into account; it is simply assumed that the farming and manufacturing interest groups exist and that they find it worthwhile to engage in the struggle about tariffs.

Other models of the political market for protection that have

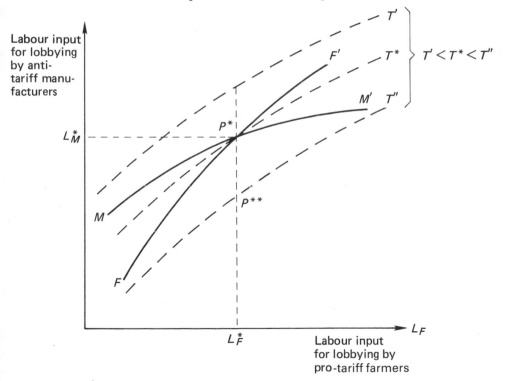

FIGURE 2.5 Lobbying equilibria and associated tariff levels.

been devised concentrate more closely on the interaction between the interest groups' demands for, and the parties' (or government's) supply of, protective measures (Brock and Magee 1978). The pressure groups 'invest' both votes and money to influence the parties' position on the free trade/protectionist issue. The more concentrated and better organized gainers from a tariff can compensate for their lower vote number by offering financial support to a party considering their wishes. The losers from a tariff usually have a larger voting strength but can muster fewer resources for their benefit. The two competing parties are compelled to maximize the probability of getting sufficient votes to come into power by using the financial resources at their disposition and by choosing an appropriate position on the free trade/protectionist issue. The more protectionist a party's position is, the more resources it will receive from the pro-tariff pressure groups. It thereby alienates, however, the anti-tariff consumer-voters (and loses some financial support from the pro-free-trade export group). A party's optimal position on the tariff issue is reached when the positive marginal effect of increased resources on the re-election probability equals the negative marginal effect of lost votes (and resource flows) from the other group. The model endogenously determines the tariff level, the amount and distribution of resources used to finance parties and the distribution of the vote between the parties. Tariffs in this framework may be considered a 'price' that equilibrates political markets.

CONCLUSION

International trade theory proves that a (unilateral) move to free trade by a country maximizes economic welfare. The corresponding welfare loss of protectionism can and has been calculated. In reality, we observe intensive bargaining and reciprocity agreements for tariff reductions. Theory and reality can be reconciled by taking into account the fact that information, transactions and bargaining are not free of cost and that not all interests are represented equally in the democratic political process.

Tariffs are decided in a *political market*; it pays to invest resources in order to gain the rents from protection. The pro-tariff groups, composed mainly of import-competing industries (capital owners, management and workers), have a strong political position because their demand for protection is clearly visible and understandable and the organizational problem is more easily manageable. The anti-tariff groups, composed mainly of consumers, find it difficult to organize effectively because of the free-riding effect. The level and structure of protection is the result of the interaction between the actors of the demand side (mostly interest groups organizing along industry lines) and the supply side (government and the civil service). This political equilibrium can be modelled in various ways.

FURTHER READING

WORKS MENTIONED IN THE TEXT

Balassa, Bela, and Kreinin, Mordechai E. (1967), 'Trade Liberalization under the Kennedy Round: The Static Effects'. *Review of Economics and Statistics*, 49 (May), 125–37.

Baldwin, Robert E. (1976), *The Political Economy of US Trade Policy*. Bulletin no. 4, Center for the Study of Financial Institutions. Graduate School of Business Administration, New York University.

Baldwin, Robert E. (1982), 'The Political Economy of Protectionism'. In Jagdish N. Bhagwati (ed.), *Import Competition and Response*. Chicago: Cambridge University Press of Chicago, 263–92.

Baldwin, Robert E., Mutti, John H. and Richardson, J. David (1980), 'Welfare Effects on the United States of a Significant Multilateral Tariff Reduction'. *Journal of International Economics*, 10 (August), 405–23.

Brock, William A. and Magee, Stephen P. (1978), 'The Economics of Special Interest Politics: The Case of the Tariff'. *American Economic Review*, 68 (May), 246–50.

Brown, Fred and Whalley, John (1980), 'General Equilibrium Evaluations of Tariff Cutting Proposals in the Tokyo Round and Comparisons with More Extensive Liberalization of World Trade'. *Economic Journal*, 90 (December), 838–66.

Easton, Stephen T. and Grubel, Herbert G. (1983), 'The Costs and Benefits of Protection in a Growing World'. *Kyklos*, 36 (fasc. 2), 213–30.

Findlay, Ronald, and Wellisz, Stanislaw (1983), 'Some Aspects of the Political Economy of Trade Restrictions'. *Kyklos*, 36 (fasc. 3), 469–81.

Finger, J. M., Hall, H. Keith and Nelson, Douglas R. (1982), 'The Political Economy of Administered Protection'. *American Economic Review*, 72 (June), 452–66.

Johnson, Harry G. (1958), 'The Gains from Freer Trade with Europe. An Estimate'. *Manchester School of Economic and Social Studies*, 26 (September), 247–55.

Johnson, Harry G. (1969), 'Optimal Trade Intervention in the Presence of Domestic Distortions'. Reprinted in Jagdish N. Bhagwati (ed.), *International Trade*. Harmondsworth: Penguin (1969), 184–217.

Magee, Stephen P. (1972), 'The Welfare Effects of Restrictions on US Trade'. *Brookings Papers on Economic Activity*, 3 (3), 645–701.

Magee, Stephen P. (1980), 'Three Simple Tests of the Stolper–Samuelson Theorem'. In Peter Oppenheimer (ed.), *Issues in International Economics*. Stockfield: Oriel Press, 138–53.

Messerlin, Patrick A. (1981), 'The Political Economy of Protectionism: The Bureaucratic Case'. *Weltwirtschaftliches Archiv*, 117, 469–96.

Stolper, Wolfgang and Samuelson, Paul (1941), 'Protection and Real Wages'. *Review of Economic Studies*, 9 (November), 58–73.

WORKS RELATING TO FURTHER ASPECTS DISCUSSED

On the practice of international trade negotiations consult, for example:

MacBean, Alasdair, I. and Snowden, P. Nicholas (1981), *International Institutions in Trade and Finance*. London: Allen and Unwin.

For another survey on measurement of the effects of tariff barriers, see:

Greenaway, David (1983), *International Trade Policy*. London: Macmillan.

Revenue-seeking is treated in:

Bhagwati, Jagdish N. and Srinivasan, T. N. (1980), 'Revenue Seeking: A Generalisation of the Theory of Tariffs'. *Journal of Political Economy*, 88 (December), 1069–87.

The original contributions are by

Krueger, Anne O. (1974), 'The Political Economy of the Rent-Seeking Society'. *American Economic Review*, 64 (June), 291–303.
Tullock, Gordon (1967), 'The Welfare Costs of Tariffs, Monopolies and Theft'. *Western Economic Journal*, 5 (June), 224–32.

A survey is provided in:
Tollison, Robert D. (1982), 'Rent Seeking: A Survey'. *Kyklos*, 35 (fasc, 4), 575–602.

3

What Determines Protectionism?
Empirical Analyses

The political economics of free trade and protection discussed in
the last chapter has been the subject of some empirical research.
So far, however, only specific aspects have been tested empirically. The studies provide interesting evidence about the
quantitative aspects of tariffs and other protective devices, and
they provide strong support of the politico-economic approach
here used. As is common practice today, econometric methods,
in particular multiple regressions, have been applied that take a
number of influences into account and are able to isolate the
contribution of each determining factor to tariff formation,
holding other influences constant.

Empirical analyses have been used both to explain the differences of protection between industries (cross-sectional) as well as
the cyclical development of protection (time-series). Various
aspects of protectionism have been studied: the political pressure
or demand exerted in the form of hearings or in parliamentary
votes – that is, the input; and the outcome of the politico-
economic struggle as reflected in tariff rates, non-tariff barriers
or, more broadly, industry assistance by government.

In this chapter, some selected econometric studies will be
presented, starting with explanations of the degree of protection
across industries and followed by explanations of the cyclical
development of protection over time.

EXPLAINING THE DIFFERENCES IN PROTECTION BETWEEN INDUSTRIES

VOTING ON TARIFFS

The behaviour of members of parliament *vis-à-vis* tariff issues has been analysed econometrically for the case of the US Congress. The study (Baldwin 1976) seeks to explain the differences in political pressure for or against protection from foreign competition between industries, and not the actual tariff level arrived at, as a result of political demand and supply. The specific issue to which *multivariate probit analysis* (a kind of multiple regression in which the dependent variable is constrained between 0 and 1) is applied is the trade-liberalizing bill introduced to the House of Representatives by a Republican president in 1973. The probability of a congressman voting *for* the trade bill (a liberal trade vote, indicated by a dummy variable taking the value 0) or *against* the trade bill (a protectionist vote, indicated by a dummy variable taking the value of 1) is explained by four determinants:

1 the proportion of import-sensitive industries in the congressman's constituency: a positive influence is expected, because the congressman has an incentive to vote against the liberalizing trade bill in order to please his voters. This means that the expected sign of the coefficient is positive, because the dummy variables standing for the vote decision have been coded, so that a higher value (1) means rejection of the bill;
2 the proportion of export-oriented industries in the congressman's constituency: the more export-oriented a constituency is, the more likely it is that the congressman will support the liberalizing trade bill, which means that a negative sign of the coefficient estimate is expected;
3 the financial contribution to the congressman's campaign made by the three major trade unions opposing the bill: as a congressman is sensitive to the size of monetary contributions received, it is expected that this will induce him to vote against the bill, so that the expected sign is positive;
4 the party affiliation: if the congressman is a Republican, a respective dummy variable takes the value 1; in the case of a

Democrat, it takes the value 0. A negative coefficient sign is expected because the bill is introduced by a Republican president.

The probit estimate yields the following equation:

Probability of supporting the 1973 trade bill

$$
\begin{aligned}
= & - 0.40 \,(\text{constant}) \\
& + 3.49^{**} \quad (\text{import-sensitive industries}) \\
& (2.62) \\
& + 1.16 \quad (\text{export-oriented industries}) \\
& (1.28) \\
& +0.0004^{**} \ (\text{union campaign contribution}) \\
& (3.22) \\
& - 1.20^{**} \quad (\text{party affiliation}) \\
& (6.79)
\end{aligned}
$$

The values in parentheses are the approximate t-values, i.e. the ratio of the maximum likelihood estimate of the coefficient divided by the standard error; the presence of one (two) asterisk(s) indicates statistical significance at the 95 (99) per cent confidence level. The explanatory variables as a whole have a statistically significant effect at the 99 per cent confidence level by the χ^2 test.

The variables relating to import-sensitive industries, trade union contributions and party affiliation are all statistically significant at the 99 per cent confidence level. As theoretically expected, the larger the weight of the industries in competition with imports in his constituency, the more likely a congressman is to yield to their pressure and to vote against the trade-liberalizing bill (the coefficient has a positive sign, because rejecting the bill is coded as 1). It is interesting to note that export-oriented industries do not have a statistically significant influence on the congressman's vote decisions; this corresponds well with the theoretical notion that anti-tariff interests are politically less influential than pro-tariff interests.

As assumed in the two theoretical models just discussed, the financial contributions – here, of protectionist trade unions – are able to influence a congressman's behaviour: the more money he gets, the more likely he is to vote against the free trade bill.

Finally, it stands to reason that, owing to party allegiance, a Republican congressman is more likely to support the trade bill introduced by a president coming from his party than is a Democratic congressman. The results of this econometric analysis of the voting behaviour in the US Congress accords very well with the political economy approach to tariff formation as set out.

ACTUAL TARIFF RATES

Several studies have analysed the differences in tariff rates between industries as the outcome of the political struggle between the demand and supply of protection.

A particularly interesting contribution to explain the tariff structure compares three competing models (Caves 1976).

1 The government sets tariffs to maximize the probability of winning the election given a geographically represented electorate ('vote maximization model').
2 Interest groups determine the structure of tariffs, the various industries having different benefits and costs of lobbying for protection ('interest group model').
3 The government sets tariffs to effect a collective nationalistic feeling about the industrial composition of the economy ('national policy model').

These three models emphasize different aspects of the politico-economic processes behind tariff-setting. They have been used to explain empirically Canada's tariff rate structure for the year 1963. A multiple regression has been run across industries (depending on data availability, the data base consists of between 29 and 35). Explanatory variables have been chosen that are intended to represent the typical features of each of the three models.

Problems arise because the operationalization of some of the theoretical variables is doubtful as adequate statistics were not always available, and because the collinearity between various variables makes it difficult to identify the direction and magnitude of their influence on tariff rates. Several of the variables included have statistically insignificant coefficients and/or have a theoretically unexpected sign.

Judged on the number of significant variables and on the presence of correct coefficient signs, the interest group model comes out best: the more low-skilled and low-wage workers are employed in an industry, the higher are the tariff rates, since the respective pressure groups have better reasons for asking for protection. When the firms buying a product are strongly concentrated, and when they are confronted with a high seller concentration, they are induced to organize more strongly and are, *ceteris paribus*, able to keep tariff rates low. The slower the growth of an industry, the more it seeks political assistance for tariff protection. This latter influence is, however, not statistically significant.

The national policy model has many signs of the coefficients as theoretically expected but suffers from a low statistical significance. It also explains the smallest share of the variance in the Canadian tariff rates (the adjusted $\bar{R}^2$ is 43 per cent, compared with over 50 per cent for the vote maximization and interest group model). In the vote maximization model several variables have the theoretically expected influence on tariff rates and are statistically significant, but this is offset by wrongly signed significant coefficients.

On the whole, the econometric tests of the three models are only partially successful. A major reason for this may be not only the problems connected with operationalization and statistical testing, but also the wrong specification of the models. In particular, the politico-economic model is identified with vote maximization, an assumption that is questionable in view of the fact that between elections, the government need not be concerned exclusively about votes; it is only at election times that it needs to muster a sufficient share of the votes in order to stay in power. It follows that the distinction between the political and the interest group model becomes doubtful, because between elections a democratically chosen government may well yield to the pressures of the organized groups, in particular because it needs their support to carry out its economic policies successfully, and also because it is interested in their financial support in view of the future elections.

An alternative interest group explanation of Canada's tariff structure stresses international political influences (Helleiner

1977). A time-series analysis for the period 1961–70 suggests that labour and multinational firms have the largest influence on tariffs: labour seeks increased protection because of the rising supply of industrial products from low-wage countries, while multinationals are interested in free trade.

Similar studies on the determinants of the tariff structure between industries have been carried out for other countries, including France, West Germany, Japan, the UK and the United States, in the context of a research project sponsored by the World Bank. The results suggest again that the import-competing industries tend to get higher tariff protection than the industries with export interests. It also turns out that labour-intensive, low-wage industries, and sectors with few firms and large numbers of employees, tend to be protected more because they can argue more convincingly in the political discussion that they are directly threatened by foreign suppliers, and, owing to the large number of voters involved, it is in the government's interest to yield to their demands for protection.

One of the most recent studies (Lavergne 1983) distinguishes three sets of determinants of the level of, and the change over a time period in, tax rates. The first is 'political', and refers to pressure group influences; the second contains 'mixed' economic and political influences, such as the effort by decision-makers to minimize displacement costs, the comparative advantage of the industry relative to foreign competition and tariff-setting as a means of international bargaining; the third set of determinants includes 'principles' such as the maintenance of historical continuity, as well as miscellaneous aspects related to a public interest view of tariff setting.

The econometric test was applied on 300 manufacturing industries in the United States from 1930 to the present. The estimates reveal that the most important influence on the tariff-setting process is conservatism: the structure of tariff rates between industries tends to be maintained over time. Of considerable importance is the possibility of using home tariffs in the international bargaining process over protectionism and free trade. It also turns out that the more competitive an industry is in the international field (the greater its comparative advantage), the lower is its tariff level. Contrary to almost all the other econometric studies of tariff formation, the pressure groups do not seem to exert any systematic influence. This rather surprising result may be due to various reasons (in particular to a mis-specification of the estimation equation and inadequate operationalization of the pressure group influence), and should not be taken too seriously. The study is, however, useful, because it shows that there is a great number of different factors that may influence the tariff-setting process.

NON-TARIFF BARRIERS

Tariffs are not the only instrument for protection from foreign competition. There exist a great many forms of non-tariff barriers to international trade, including any government practice that has the effect of discriminating between foreign and domestic goods. A survey of the US Tariff Commission (1974) has brought to light over 4500 complaints about non-tariff barriers. Table 3.1 lists the five main types of such barriers and the percentage share of the complaints falling in these categories. By far the most important non-tariff barriers are the quantity restrictions imposed by governments (with over 35 per cent of the total), and non-tariff import burdens (with just under 30 per cent of the total).

TABLE 3.1   Complaints about non-tariff barriers to international trade according to categories, 1974

Category of non-tariff barriers	Percentage distribution
	%
Non-tariff burdens on imports	29
Quantity restrictions	36
Government participation in international trade	12
Technical norms, standards and rules of consumer protection	11
Administrative restrictions	12
Total	100
	($N = 4558$)

Source: Own compilations, based on US Tariff Commission (1974).

An explanation of the typical features of non-tariff barriers may be based on the economic theory of regulation (see, e.g., Peltzman 1976). This argues that the regulators serve special interest groups. Government intervention in a market may be viewed as a politically optimal way for redistributing wealth from some constituents to others. When an outside interference takes place, the regulatory interventions have to be changed in order to re-establish political equilibrium. In the international trade area one such intervention was the Kennedy Round, the purpose of which was to reduce tariffs across the board by 50 per cent – the so-called 'linear rule'. The negotiations were quite successful. The simple average tariff reduction on US manufacturing products was 46.8 per cent between 1967 and 1972. The share of imports in domestic sales of manufactured products rose from an average of 4.8 per cent in 1967 to 7.3 per cent in 1972.

However, if the linear rule envisioned in the Kennedy Round had materialized, the largest cut in absolute terms should have come in those economic sectors with highest trade barriers. This did not in fact occur. The tariff reductions were systematic and were not uniform across industries, and the substantial reductions of the average tariff level did not have the expected effect on the structure of imports into the United States. An important further reason why the structure of imports was not strongly affected by the Kennedy Round was that the tariff reduction was substituted by other forms of protection, in particular by regulatory non-tariff barriers.

This theory of the interaction of tariffs and non-tariff barriers to international trade has been empirically tested for the year 1970 (when most of the Kennedy Round reductions had already materialized) (Marvel and Ray 1983). Theoretically we would expect that the tariff rates existing in that year would be higher (and consequently that the tariff cuts had been smaller) in those US industries that:

1 were declining, and whose consumers were therefore forced by regulations to share in their ill fortune;
2 were concentrated, and hence able to organize to maintain protection;

3 were composed mainly of firms selling to consumers, who find it difficult to organize against protectionism;

4 were internationally not very competitive. In other words, tariff cuts can be expected to have been larger in those US industries that were internationally more competitive, in particular the high-technology producers.

Another explanatory variable is the 'historically given' tariff rate of 1965, which indicates the political equilibrium before the tariff cuts of the Kennedy Round.

Non-tariff barriers are expected to be used either to offset the impact of painful tariff reductions, or to augment protection in industries where international competition is most troublesome. Consequently, some of the same factors are expected to determine the relative intensity of non-tariff barriers as determine the tariff rates across industries, in particular the concentration of firms in an industry and the weakness of the opposition. Because the increase in non-tariff barriers is seen (partly) as a reaction to the Kennedy Round of tariff reductions, the *change* in tariffs between 1965 and 1970 is introduced as an additional explanatory variable, with a negative coefficient sign expected.

The results of the econometric estimates of the determinants of US tariff rates and non-tariff barriers across 261 manufacturing industries are shown in table 3.2. The estimation equation for tariff rates is able to explain statistically 78 per cent of the variance of tariff rates across industries ($\bar{R}^2$). All the coefficients are statistically significant and have the theoretically expected signs. The results show that US manufacturing industries experiencing rapid growth are likely to have less protection than declining industries. High-concentration industries are more successful in organizing opposition against tariff reductions and therefore have relatively high tariffs. Industries selling primarily to consumers are also better able to avoid tariff reductions, while internationally competitive (high-technology) industries have to cope with relatively little protection (low tariffs). The respective tariff reductions within the Kennedy Round have been used primarily to achieve parallel reductions in foreign tariffs, i.e. for negotiation purposes.

TABLE 3.2 Determinants of tariff rates and non-tariff barriers in US manufacturing, 1970

Explanatory variables	Coefficient estimates* (t-ratios in parentheses)	
	Tariff rates	Non-tariff barriers
Growth rate of industry (percentage change in total employment, 1958–67)	−5.19** (−4.46)	——
Degree of concentration (share of four largest firms in the industry)	0.03* (2.19)	−0.01** (−2.47)
Weakness of opposition (consumer goods ratio)	2.05* (2.08)	0.78** (2.76)
International competitiveness (share of high-technology production, measured by percentage of scientists and engineers in total employment)	−17.06** (−4.24)	——
Historical tariff rate (1965)	0.60** (21.9)	0.03 (2.33)
Change in tariffs (1965–70) (percentage point)	——	0.03** (1.94)
Constant	6.34	
R^2	78%	

*One (two) asterisks indicates statistical significance at the 95 (99) per cent confidence level.
Source: Marvel and Ray (1983); compilation from tables 1 and 2.

Consider now the estimation for non-tariff barriers in table 3.2. This confirms that they are related to the historical political equilibrium before the Kennedy Round (in the form of the tariff rate of 1965). The coefficient on the tariff change variable is not statistically different from zero at the customary levels of confidence. The theoretically expected negative sign does not materialize, which suggests that there is not only a substitutive, but also a complementary effect between tariffs and non-tariff barriers; those industries having the highest tariff protection also have the political influence necessary to obtain high non-tariff protection.

The two forms of protection, however, are not equally attractive for specific industries. The estimates indicate that non-tariff barriers are more accessible than tariffs for low-concentration industries. (The coefficients for non-tariff barriers and tariff rates are negative and positive, respectively, which means that, the higher the degree of concentration, the more accessible is tariff protection.) The low-concentration industries have greater difficulties in obtaining political influence, mainly because of the free-rider problem. For firms in industries with a great number of suppliers, the rents generated by tariffs cannot easily be appropriated because they may be bid away through the rapid entry of new domestic firms into the industry. Non-tariff barriers are more advantageous because the rents generated can often be distributed selectively to punish free-riders, and can be withheld from new entrants. Import quotas based on historic sales of the firms already in the market are an example.

Finally, the estimates shown in table 3.2 suggest that both tariffs and non-tariff barriers tend to be high in consumer goods industries, because the consumers who are burdened therewith find it difficult to organize themselves effectively. On the whole, the estimates strongly support the political economy interpretation of the process of protectionism. They indicate that there is a systematic influence of special interests which undermines the linear type of trade liberalization agreed to in such agreements as the Kennedy Round. It is shown that the factors that make it possible for some industries to gain more protection than others can be empirically identified.

VOLUNTARY EXPORT RESTRAINTS

In recent years, international trade relations have witnessed the emergence and rapid expansion of voluntary export restraints as an additional tool of protection to tariffs and non-tariff barriers. These barriers to trade are introduced by the exporting country, usually in order to avoid harsher measures by the importing country, such as prohibitively high tariffs or very low import quotas. Voluntary export restraints are the result of a bargain between the exporting and importing countries, and are 'voluntary' only in so far as they are not (directly) imposed by the importing country. They have been applied to a large number of manufacturing goods, such as steel, colour television sets and motor cars.

Voluntary export restraints differ in three main respects from global tariffs or global non-tariff barriers:

1 They are discriminatory, lowering the import share of restraining exporters.
2 They lead to a deterioration in the importing country's terms of trade. The prices of the imported goods concerned rise because of the supply restrictions. The rents created by the price increases are appropriated by the restraining exporters.
3 The agreements are reached in clandestine governmental consultations.

These three characteristics offer specific incentives to certain decision-makers to favour such export restraints (see Jones 1984). The government and public bureaucracy in the importing country find it a suitable instrument by which to achieve protectionist ends at a low political cost. Being 'voluntarily' agreed to by exporters, they do not violate international trade agreements such as the GATT restrictions on trade barriers. They are targeted at 'disruptive' suppliers, so that no retaliation has to be feared by other suppliers. (On the contrary, as they reduce the competition of the most efficient suppliers, the other suppliers reap the benefit.) Voluntary export restraints are quickly implemented and are in the hands of the government and its administration, while parliament need not be consulted.

The import-competing domestic producers reap the normal benefits from this type of protection. They receive rents by being able to raise the prices of the (smaller number of) imported goods and increase their own output. They are not easily made responsible for the cost of such protection because the attention is focused on the foreign exports, which are said to have 'disrupted' the market. Voluntary export restraints are also beneficial to the foreign exporting firms, because the reduction in exports creates monopoly rents which they can appropriate (provided that exporters from other countries do not compensate for the reduction – which, however, would be prevented by the importing country by further voluntary export restraint agreements).

In order to implement a voluntary export restraint agreement, the foreign government must set up an export cartel which tends to favour the established firms in the economic sector concerned. Competition is weakened by the allocation of export market shares, and the entry of new firms is prevented. The consumers in the importing country are the group that has to carry the burden, as with all other kinds of protection from international competition. In this case, they have to pay twice: once in the form of higher domestic prices, and again in the form of foregone tariff revenues. Consumers are excluded from the decision-making process; the agreements are negotiated by highly specialized experts on a technical level, removed from the public view.

The costs involved by such voluntary agreements are not only difficult to understand and to measure quantitatively, but also are (so far) not part of the political debate in which the opponents of this form of protectionism can, or are willing to, raise their voices. For these reasons it is not surprising that this new protectionist tool has gained in importance as a substitute for more open, and politically sensitive, protectionism by tariffs.

EXPLAINING THE CYCLICAL DEVELOPMENT OF PROTECTION

Protectionism is strongest when a country's economic position is weak; attempts at liberalizing international trade have the best chances when economic conditions are good. These statements are almost commonplace; the question is, however, whether they are supported by serious empirical analyses. In this section studies are discussed that inquire as to whether low levels of economic activity, high unemployment, worsening trade deficits and increasing import penetration do indeed increase the temptation to protect domestic industries from import competition.

NUMBER OF 'ESCAPE CLAUSE' PETITIONS TO THE ITC

One way to measure the intensity of the demand for protection is the number of 'escape clause' petitions to the International Trade

Commission under the trade legislation of the United States. It may be hypothesized that the number of such petitions is larger:

1 the worse domestic economic conditions are (measured by the level of the gross national product, unemployment or unused capacity), because the industries threatened by foreign competition can establish a 'convincing case' that the bad state of the economy is due to 'unfair' competition by foreign suppliers. This raises the expected rate of return for political activity, and the managers and labour representatives are induced to switch part of their activity away from the area of low-returns economic production;
2 the worse the balance of trade is, as an indicator of the (unsatisfactory) international competitive position of the country;
3 the larger import penetration is, because this is an obvious sign the domestic industries can point to in order to 'prove' the damaging influence of foreign suppliers;
4 the larger the number of successful escape clause petitions has been in recent years, because a firm considering making a petition takes this as a favourable element in its benefit–cost comparison.

Table 3.3 presents the econometric estimates based on data covering the 30 years 1949–79 (Takacs 1981). As some of the explanatory variables are highly correlated, estimates are presented in which one of the correlated variables is excluded in turn.

The results of the estimates support the theoretical hypothesis: macroeconomic conditions significantly affect protectionist pressures. The number of escape clause cases rises the lower the level of real GNP, the higher the unemployment rate and the lower capacity utilization are. Foreign trade conditions also have the expected influence: the worse the trade balance (exports minus imports) and the greater import penetration are, the more petitions will be filed demanding protection. Finally, the larger the share of petitions that were successful in the past, the more new ones will be made, *ceteris paribus*.

TABLE 3.3   Determinants of the number of US escape clause petitions to the international trade commission, 1949–79

Explanatory variables	Coefficient estimates* (t-values in parentheses) Equations		
	(1)	(2)	(3)
Gross national product (real)	−0.01** (−4.24)	−0.02** (−4.21)	−0.009** (−3.73)
Rate of unemployment	1.42** (2.88)		1.32* (2.65)
Capacity utilization		−0.37** (−2.95)	
Trade balance	−0.17* (−2.28)		
Import penetration		190.9** (3.28)	
Success rate of recent petitions			9.39* (2.20)
Constant	10.49	43.85	6.37
R^2	44%	56%	43%

*One (two) asterisks indicate(s) statistical significance at the 95 (99) per cent confidence level.
Source: Takacs (1981); selection from table 1.

DUMPING CASES

In another study (Magee 1982) the protectionist pressure is measured by the number of dumping cases filed with the US Bureau of Customs: the (prospective or actual) losses incurred by import-competing firms cause them to file charges of dumping against foreign exporters. Protectionist pressure is again hypo-thesized to rise with unemployment. Increasing inflation, on the other hand, leads to pressure from households and consumer groups to liberalize imports.

The econometric estimate with annual data from 1933 to 1979 yields the following result:

$$\log (\text{protection}) = \quad - 0.15 \quad \text{(constant)}$$

$$+ 0.92^{**} \quad \log (\text{unemployment, per cent})$$
$$(6.77)$$
$$- 5.67^{**} \quad \text{(inflation, per cent)}$$
$$(3.88)$$
$$- 1.38^{**} \quad \text{(dummy variable)}$$
$$(7.54)$$
$$R^2 = 0.72$$

The figures in parentheses are the t-values. The dummy variable takes the value 1 for 1933–52, and 0 for 1953–77, to account for an (unexplained) structural shift.

The coefficients for unemployment and inflation have the expected positive and negative signs and are statistically significant. A 10 per cent increase in the rate of unemployment (e.g. from 5 to 5.5 per cent) is associated with a 9 per cent increase in protectionist pressure; each percentage point rise in the rate of inflation (e.g. from 7 to 8 per cent) lowers the protectionist pressure by 5.7 per cent.

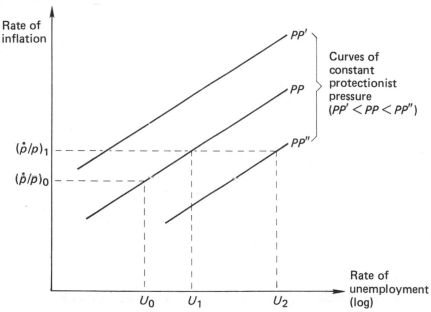

FIGURE 3.1 Protection pressure as produced by unemployment and inflation.

Figure 3.1 shows the locus of constant protectionist pressure, which has a positive slope: the demands for a rise in tariffs will be the same with low unemployment and low inflation (that is, U_0 and $(\dot{p}/p)_0$ produce PP) and with high unemployment and high inflation (U_1 and $(\dot{p}/p)_1$ again produce pressure PP). However, an increasing rate of unemployment (e.g. from U_1 to U_2) and constant inflation (e.g. $(\dot{p}/p)_1$) produce a higher pressure for protection (PP''). The figure shows three lines of constant protectionist pressure; the lower and further to the right such a line is located, the higher is the pressure for protectionism.

The econometric estimates of the cyclical influences on the tariff formation process are so far limited to the demand side. The difficulty is, of course, to find a sufficiently long and comparable data series to perform a similar type of analysis on actual tariffs or on other protectionist measures as the outcome of the political struggle.

CONCLUSION

The unequal degree of protection of the various industries against foreign competition in the politico-economic process has been analysed by econometric methods, considering the demand side (voting on tariffs) and the political equilibrium outcome (actual tariff rates). Non-tariff barriers can be explained empirically by a similar set of determinants, because the two means of protection are used partly as substitutes. Tariffs and non-tariff barriers are found to be linked positively with the importance and degree of concentration of import-competing industries. Declining industries, and sectors with low-skilled, low-wage employees in large numbers have a good chance of getting protection. The more competitive an industry is (among them the multinational firms), the lower, *ceteris paribus*, is protection. Important influences on tariffs and non-tariff barriers are also the historically given structure of protection and the possibilities for international bargaining. As theoretically expected, the export-oriented industries and consumers have little or no influence on issues of free trade and protection.

Recently, voluntary export restraints have become important as a protectionist device. These are advantageous for both the

home industry and the foreign suppliers (the latter can appropriate the monopoly rents of curtailed supply), as well as for the
government and public bureaucracy, mainly because there is no
possibility and incentive for consumers (who carry the burden) to
oppose such agreements.

Protectionism is empirically shown to be strongest when a
country's economic conditions are weak, in particular if GNP is
low and unemployment high, and when the foreign trade position
is bad. Rising inflation, on the other hand, leads to a pressure to
reduce tariffs.

The econometric studies presented provide, on the whole,
strong support for the political economy of protection.

FURTHER READING

WORKS MENTIONED IN THE TEXT

Baldwin, Robert E. (1976), *The Political Economy of US Postwar Trade Policy*. Bulletin no. 4, Centre for the Study of Financial Institutions. Graduate School of Business Administration, New York University.
Caves, Richard E. (1976), 'Economic Models of Political Choice: Canada's Tariff Structure'. *Canadian Journal of Economics*, 9 (May), 278–300.
Helleiner, Gerald K. (1977), 'The Political Economy of Canada's Tariff Structure: An Alternative Model'. *Canadian Journal of Economics*, 10 (May), 318–36.
Jones, Kent (1984), 'The Political Economy of Voluntary Export Restraint Agreements'. *Kyklos*, 37 (1), 82–101.
Lavergne, Réal P. (1983), *The Political Economy of US Tariffs. An Empirical Analysis*. Toronto: Academic Press.
Magee, Stephen P. (1982), 'Protectionism in the United States'. Department of Finance, University of Texas at Austin, mimeo.
Marvel, Howard P. and Ray, Edward J. (1983), 'The Kennedy Round: Evidence on the Regulation of International Trade in the United States'. *American Economic Review*, 75 (March), 190–7.
Peltzman, Sam (1976), 'Toward a More General Theory of Regulation'. *Journal of Law and Economics*, 19 (August), 211–40.
Takacs, Wendy E. (1981), 'Pressures for Protectionism: An Empirical Analysis'. *Economic Inquiry*, 19 (October), 687–93.
US Tariff Commission (1974), *Trade Barriers: An Overview*, Vol. 4. Washington DC: US Government Printing Office.

WORKS RELATING TO FURTHER ASPECTS DISCUSSED

A forerunner to the empirical analysis of the determinants of protection is

Schattschneider, Elmar E. (1935), *Politics, Pressures, and the Tariff*. Englewood Cliffs, NJ: Prentice Hall.

Schattschneider advanced the idea that the tariff obtained by an industry is a function of the degree of pressure the industry is able to organize. His empirical analysis relates to the politics surrounding tariff formation in the United States. The public hearings held by Congress are used as indicators for political pressure.

Another early champion of the interest group approach is

Kindleberger, Charles P. (1951), 'Group Behaviour and International Trade'. *Journal of Political Economy*, 59 (February), 30–46.

Kindleberger illustrates his approach mainly by historical examples.

One of the first econometric studies has been used to explain the US tariff structure of 1824, again based on a pressure group process:

Pincus, Jonathan J. (1975), 'Pressure Groups and the Pattern of Tariffs'. *Journal of Political Economy*, 83 (July/August), 757–78.

A survey of the World Bank studies on tariff rates across industries is provided in

Anderson, Kym and Baldwin, Robert E. (1981), 'The Political Market for Protection in Industrial Countries: Empirical Evidence'. *World Bank Staff Working Paper* no. 492 (October).

Non-tariff barriers are extensively treated in

Baldwin, Robert E. (1970), *Nontariff Distortions of International Trade*. Washington: Brookings Institution.

In the respective studies for Germany and Italy it was shown that internationally negotiated tariff reductions were substituted by increased non-tariff barriers.

4

How Risky is Foreign Investment?

DEEP CONCERN ABOUT LENDING IN THE 1980s

In March 1981, Poland declared that it simply did not have the $2.5 billion due to its creditors that year to service its more than $25 billion debt. In August 1982, Mexico announced that it was unable to meet payments on its debt of $80 billion. Soon afterwards, Brazil made it clear that it could not come up with the interest on its debt of $90 billion.

At the end of 1982, the total debt held by banks, governments and international financial institutions against developing and Eastern bloc countries was estimated to be more than $700 billion (but it is not quite clear how large the debt really is). The mass of this debt is concentrated on a few nations: among the developing countries on Brazil, Mexico, Argentina, the Republic of Korea, Venezuela and Israel; among the Communist countries on Poland, the Soviet Union, Yugoslavia and East Germany. Table 4.1 shows estimates of the overall indebtedness of selected developing and Eastern bloc countries at the end of 1982. The sum of the debt of the six developing countries listed amounts to $305 billion, which is almost half (44 per cent) of the estimated total debt of $700 billion. The table shows that Poland and the Soviet Union have accumulated a sizeable debt, amounting to around $25 billion each.

Such absolute figures are difficult to comprehend. It is more useful to set the debt service payments in a given year (which includes interest and amortization) against the country's total export receipts in order to gain a better idea of the magnitudes involved. This 'debt service ratio' is estimated to be 155 per cent for Argentina, 125 per cent for Mexico and Israel, 120 per cent

TABLE 4.1   Overall indebtedness of selected developing and eastern bloc countries: estimates for end 1982

Country	Debt amount outstanding	Debt service/ export ratio
	($ billion)	(%)
Selected developing countries		
Brazil	90	120
Mexico	80	125
Argentina	45	155
Republic of Korea	35	50
Venezuela	30	100
Israel	25	125
Selected Eastern bloc countries		
Poland	26	95
USSR	23	25
German Democratic Republic	14	85

Source: Herbert Wilkens, 'The Debt Burden of Developing Countries'. *Economics*, 28(1983) Table 2; selected and rounded figures.

for Brazil and 95 per cent for Poland. As may be seen from the table, the debt service/export ratio is much lower for other heavy borrowers, such as the Republic of Korea (50 per cent) and the Soviet Union (25 per cent).

In view of the huge indebtedness, and the difficulties of repayment, there is grave concern among all international financial institutions, be they private (such as commercial banks) or public (such as central banks and the International Monetary Fund). Compared with the past, there has been a dramatic change over a short period. The international debt referred to above, estimated now to be over $700 billion, was a little over $100 billion only ten years ago. This dramatic increase (even when allowing for inflation) is shown in figure 4.1.

It can be seen that the lending record was good up to quite recently. Actually, the loan losses have been far *lower* for international than for domestic lending. For the ten largest American banks (only for these are there reliable statistics)

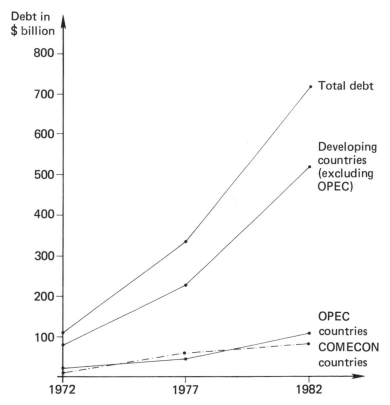

FIGURE 4.1 The development of international indebtedness, 1972–82. (*Source:* compilation from various publications by OECD, World Bank and the Bank for International Settlements.)

international net loan losses were only 0.10 per cent of average international loans in 1980. These losses were just 15 per cent of the total losses these banks incurred through their lending to domestic and foreign creditors (Group of Thirty 1982, p. 7). However, such statistics do not take into account the indirect cost to lenders of rescheduling the loans, including the time and effort devoted by management to the problem and the increased reserves the banks have to hold to maintain their liquidity.

FOREIGN DIRECT INVESTMENT

Bank lending is only one form of financial flow into developing countries. Another important flow is private direct investment;

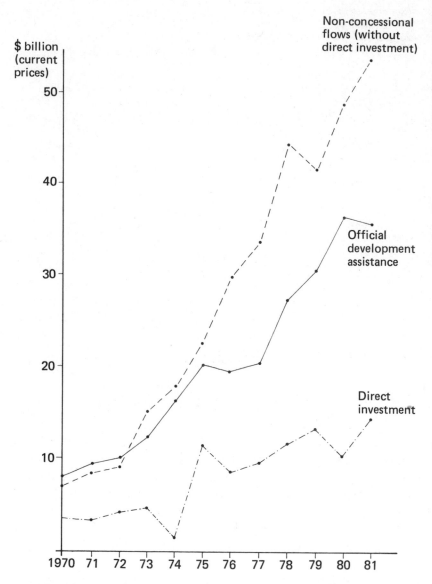

FIGURE 4.2 Net financial flows to the developing countries.
(*Source:* OECD, Development Co-operation, 1982 Review.)

this is a form of private foreign capital formation in firms so that the investor keeps a significant degree of control. A third important financial flow is foreign aid, a topic discussed in the next chapter. The growth of these three financial flows to developing countries during the 1970s is shown in figure 4.2.

This figure shows a considerable increase of all three financial flows in 1970–81, with a growing importance of bank lending and similar non-concessional flows (such as private and official export credits). Foreign direct investment rose from $3.7 billion in 1970 to more than $14 billion in 1981.

Risk is associated not only with lending of money but also with foreign direct investment. An obvious danger is nationalization without any (or with inadequate) compensation. The most spectacular nationalizations were in Russia after 1917, in Mexico in the late 1930s, in Eastern Europe and China after 1945 and, more recently, of the US oil companies in the Middle East by Arab countries, and in Cuba by Castro.

Table 4.2 shows the stock of foreign direct investment by origin; that is, it indicates by which nations the investment has been undertaken. In 1978 by far the greatest amount is attributed to the United States ($168 billion); the UK has a stock that is only one-quarter as large ($41 billion). Other countries, such as

TABLE 4.2　Stock of foreign direct investment: some of the most important countries, by origin and by destination, 1978

Country of origin	($ billion)	Country of destination	($ billion)
United States	168	Canada	43
United Kingdom	41	United States	41
Federal Republic of		United Kingdom	32
Germany	32	Federal Republic of	
Switzerland	28	Germany	29
Japan	27	Brazil	14
Netherlands	24	Mexico	6
France	15	Indonesia	6
Canada	14	Venezuela	3

Source: United Nations Centre on Transnational Corporations. Not all of the (rounded) figures include reinvested earnings.

Germany, Japan and Switzerland, have about one-sixth each of the holdings of US multinationals.

Table 4.2 also shows the stock of foreign direct investment by destination; that is, it indicates into what countries the investment funds have gone. It may be seen that a considerable foreign-owned stock of investment exists in such highly industrialized countries as the United States, Canada, the Federal Republic of Germany and the UK. Among the developing countries, the largest recipients are Brazil, Mexico, Indonesia and Venezuela. The United Nations (1983, p. 58) estimated the stock of foreign direct investment in the LDCs as $32 billion in 1967 and $88 billion in 1978. Though this stock has been growing less rapidly than the stock of foreign debt, it still represents a significant quantity of resources.

Multinational corporations have become important actors in the international politico-economic system. Considering purely their budgets in 1978, 40 of the 100 biggest units in the world were corporations: General Motors' sales surpassed the GNP of Yugoslavia (Kudrle and Bobrow 1982, p. 353).

In this chapter the emphasis will be on the effects of risk on foreign direct investment, following the general line of putting the real (as against the monetary) aspects of international political economics foremost. However, the approaches used to measure and evaluate risk are quite similar, for international financial and direct investments, to those for exports.

COUNTRY RISK

The risk faced by an international capital investment, loan or export sale arising from the character of the social and political relations existing in the recipient country, and the implied possibility of expropriation of the investment, default on the loan or failure to pay for the export, is called 'country' or 'international' risk. This risk is above and beyond that existing in the domestic market; it is generated by political entities beyond the donor country's national jurisdiction. It is often associated with the actions of national governments which interfere with the activities of wholly or partially foreign-owned business property.

Three main types of causes for country risk may be distinguished:

1 economic causes, arising from changes in property rights (such as nationalization, forced increase of the share of domestic stock owners or forced sale) and lack of foreign exchange as a consequence of natural catastrophes (such as droughts);
2 political causes arising within the recipient country, which may be legal (such as government crises, work disputes and strikes, change of foreign trade rules) or illegal (such as riots, civil war, revolutions, secessions or *coups d'état*);
3 political causes emanating from outside the recipient country, such as intervention by external powers, blockades, border disputes or a full-scale war.

In a mail survey, managers of relatively large (sales of $100 million or more in 1976) industrial and internationally oriented US-based firms (Kobrin 1982) were presented with a list of nine aspects of the political environment and were asked to select the four they considered the most important. The result is shown in table 4.3. Political instability and the investment climate were selected by a large majority (80 per cent in each case) of the 190 respondents. Remittance restrictions (70 per cent) and taxation

TABLE 4.3 International company managers' evaluation of the four most important aspects of the political environment, 1978 ($N = 190$)

Aspect	(%)
Political instability	80
Investment climate	80
Remittance restrictions	70
Taxation	51
Expropriation	28
Attitudes of political parties	24
Labour disruptions	21
Administrative restrictions	16
Public sector competition	13

Source: Kobrin (1982), table 7–1, p. 115.

(51 per cent) were also considered a very important aspect of the political environment.

Obviously, each cause may influence country risk in a quite different way and to a different extent.

Empirical evidence on the importance of the most glaring form of risk – forced divestment, also referred to as nationalization, socialization or confiscation – is rather scant. Divestment extends from formal expropriation, or forced sales to domestic subjects, to contract renegotiation, which makes it difficult to measure.

The most extensive empirical study of divestment analyses 1500 expropriations in 76 less developed countries over the period 1960–76 (Kobrin 1980). Somewhat surprisingly, this study finds that there are few cases of 'mass expropriations' in which complete foreign firms are taken after a major political change; such nationalizations took place, for example, in Tanzania (1967), Algeria (1967–72), Chile (1971–2), Ethiopia (1975), Angola and Mozambique (1975–6). But by far the largest part of all divestments (89 per cent) that occurred in this sample were undertaken selectively, as a means of furthering specific internal social and economic goals. Accordingly, firms and various economic sectors have been affected quite differently. There is a (relatively) high risk of expropriations for banking and insurance, the natural resources and the infrastructural (e.g. railways) sectors. The danger of expropriation is lower in the manufacturing and trade sectors, particularly if they are globally integrated and/or research-intensive. This is because the LDCs concerned know that they will find it difficult or impossible to manage such firms themselves. Overall, the study finds that, in the period considered, roughly 5 per cent of foreign firms have actually been expropriated in the less developed countries. M. L. Williams (1975) estimates that about 20 per cent of the *value* of foreign investment made during the period 1956–72 was expropriated without compensation.

According to the figures presented, the general risk of being expropriated is not very high. The probability of losing one's foreign direct investment depends strongly on specific factors, such as the particular countries investing and invested in, as well as the time period and sector invested in. It follows that it is particularly important to evaluate carefully the particular risk of a foreign direct investment.

At present two main avenues for assessing and measuring risk are used.

The first, and most commonly used, approach is to rely on expert opinion. Besides rather unstructured methods, which more or less randomly consider the intuitive views about country risk by (sometimes self-appointed) experts, there are more systematic efforts. The best known of these seems to be the BERI (Business Environment Risk Index), which has been computed quarterly since 1972 and covers 45 countries. The index is based on surveys among a permanent panel of over 100 volunteers from industrial firms, banks, governments and other institutions. Each panellist rates five to ten countries for a period of six to twelve months. They assign by judgment a score of 0 to 4 to each of 15 factors considered relevant for country risk. Examples of factors are political stability; attitude towards foreign direct investment; balance of payments; bureaucratic delays; quality of local management and partners; etc. The 15 factors are weighted according to what is deemed their relative importance for the business climate. The weight attributed to 'political stability' for example, is 12 per cent; to 'attitude to foreign investors and profits', 6 per cent; to 'threat of nationalization', also 6 per cent; and to the extent of handicaps imposed by 'bureaucracy', 4 per cent. While the index is quite systematic, both the rating by experts and the weighting are extremely subjective.

Various other risk indices are computed on similar principles. An example is the country rating established by the *Institutional Investor Journal*. This Institutional Investor Credit Rating Index has been calculated since 1979, and is updated every six months. It is based on a survey among 75–100 international banks. The replies are kept strictly confidential, and no bank is permitted to rate its home country. The bankers grade each foreign country on a scale between 0 and 100: the least creditworthy country with the greatest chance of default is graded 0; the most creditworthy is graded 100. It is thought that this country risk index can be applied not only to bank loans, but also to foreign direct investment. The individual responses are weighted by a formula that gives greater weight to responses from banks with the most worldwide exposure and the most sophisticated country analysis systems.

Table 4.4 presents this country risk index for a particular

TABLE 4.4   Institutional investor credit rating index of selected countries, September 1983

Group	Rank	Individual	Credit ranking (0, least creditworthy; 100, most creditworthy)
Top ten	1	United States	96
	2	Switzerland	95
	3	Japan	95
	4	German Federal Republic	94
	5	United Kingdom	89
	6	Canada	87
	7	Norway	86
	8	Netherlands	85
	9	Australia	85
	10	Austria	82
Other	18	Italy	71
selected	22	Taiwan	68
countries	24	China	63
	28	Soviet Union	61
	31	South Korea	56
	51	Brazil	38
	60	Mexico	34
	70	Argentina	28
	100	Poland	7
Bottom	103	El Salvador	6
five	104	Zaire	6
	105	Nicaragua	6
	106	North Korea	4
	107	Uganda	4
Overall average			41

Source: Institutional Investor, September 1983, p. 292.

time (September 1983). It shows the ten countries rated most creditworthy and the five countries considered least creditworthy. In between these extremes, the ratings of selected other countries are presented. The most creditworthy countries are the United States, Switzerland, Japan and West Germany, with a rating of over 90. The countries recently experiencing difficulties with debt servicing have credit ratings of 38 for Brazil, 34 for Mexico, 28 for Argentina, and as low as 7 for Poland. The countries for which the bankers judge the credit risk to be the highest are El Salvador, Zaire, Nicaragua, North Korea and Uganda, with an index of 6 or less.

The second approach to risk assessment builds on the quantitative research of past data, thus making an effort to provide a more objective base for measurement. A huge number of data (up to 400 variables) are collected and their relationship is statistically explored. A typical example (Rummel and Heenan 1978) seeks to extract four independent dimensions of risk: domestic instability, foreign conflicts, political climate and economic climate. The variables making up these dimensions are selected by purely statistical criteria, namely those variables that are most closely correlated with each other (cluster analysis). The disadvantage of this approach is that 'intuitive', non-measurable (or rather: *not yet* measured), factors are not included. Moreover, some of the variables refer to periods so far back that they are of limited relevance for measuring current country risk.

The 'expert' and the 'quantitative' approaches to risk assessment are basically deficient for the same reason: they do not have a well developed theoretical framework. The experts in the intuitive approach usually have *some* notion about what causes country risk, but this remains implicit. The quantitative approach solely exploits statistical regularities and is thus a typical example of 'measurement without theory'. In order to make progress, it is necessary to look at the *behaviour* of the actors involved (What makes a government of a LDC resort to expropriations? How do the threatened foreign firms react?), as well as at the precise effect of economic and political instability on the present value of the foreign property invested (Do government changes always increase the country risk? How far do riots in the street affect business activity?).

DETERMINANTS OF FOREIGN DIRECT INVESTMENT

That the distribution of foreign direct investment depends on both economic and political determinants would appear to be obvious. A country in which there is political unrest or in which there is a threat of having the investment nationalized without adequate compensation is more of a risk and therefore, *ceteris paribus*, less attractive to invest in than a country offering political stability and a guarantee of property rights. It is perhaps surprising that the empirical literature investigating the determinants of foreign direct investment deals only insufficiently with this joint influence of economic and political factors.

TYPES OF APPROACH

It is useful to distinguish between three types of approach, which are dubbed 'Much politics, little economics' (approach A); 'Much economics, little politics' (approach B); and 'Unstructured amalgamation of economics and politics' (approach C), in order to indicate what each approach takes to be the most important determinants of foreign direct investment.

Much politics, little economics (A)

One of the most prominent studies about the determinants of foreign direct investment (Green 1972) concentrates on the question of whether political instability has a deterrent effect, as claimed in survey studies according to which executives report political instability to be the most important variable influencing their foreign investment decisions, aside from market potential. Surprisingly, Green finds that the allocation of US foreign direct marketing investment is *not* affected by political instability in the recipient countries.

Another major study concentrating on the influence of political instability (Thunell 1977) tests the hypothesis that investments in a country decrease when it is unstable and increase when it is stable. This study finds that (1) political events, and therefore instability, are not directly associated with short-term fluctuations, but only with trend changes, in foreign investment flows; (2) the relationship is asymmetric; that is, the investing companies do not react in the exact opposite way when a country becomes more stable as when it becomes less stable. While a large number of statistical tests are made, Thunell is not able to develop a regression equation in which a variety of economic and political determinants are simultaneously included, and can be controlled for when the effect of political instability is tested.

Much economics, little politics (B)

The majority of studies dealing quantitatively with the determinants of foreign direct investment concentrate on economic factors. Political influences are either completely disregarded, or are treated as an unimportant side factor. These 'economic' studies do not provide a coherent picture; it appears that each author introduces those determinants into his regression equations that he finds personally appealing.

An eclectic theory of international direct investment based on the theories of industrial organization, of location and of the firm is developed by Dunning (1981). His general proposition is that a country's enterprises are more likely to engage in international production

1 the more ownership-specific advantages (relative to enterprises of other nationalities) are possessed;
2 the greater the incentive the firms have to internalize rather than externalize these specific advantages;
3 the more the enterprises are interested in exploiting these advantages from a foreign location.

A theory of a cycle of outward and inward investment flows composed of four stages is developed, with the purpose of explaining how these three factors depend on the level of economic development and on the structural conditions (e.g. the extent of industrialization) of the countries. For the purpose of formal statistical testing, the 67 countries (period 1967–78) are divided into three groups by cluster analysis, the dominant influence being GNP per capita. The groups of countries are then subjected to stepwise multiple regression analysis in order to determine the most important organization, internalization and location variables for outward, inward and *net* outward investment flows. The organizational variables consist of human capital (measured by skill levels) and of expenditures of research and development; the internalizational variables consist of the royalties and other fees received by local enterprises from unaffiliated firms as a percentage of such fees received from foreign affiliated and unaffiliated firms; the locational variables consist of the average hourly earnings, the growth of output, an infrastructural index, tax burden and the Business Environmental Risk Index (BERI) (see p. 69 above).

The result of Dunning's analysis does not reveal a clear structure because different variables have a statistically significant influence, depending on the country cluster and the direction of the investment flow. While the location factors are statistically significant in many cases, the Environmental Risk Index, which captures political risk, never is. Dunning's statistical analysis thus suggests that international investment flows are influenced by economic but not by political factors.

The contributions discussed so far all relate to foreign direct investment in *developing* countries (except for Dunning, 1981, which does primarily but also includes some industrialized countries). There is also a large literature on direct investment in developed countries. These studies are of limited interest for our purposes as they do not include any political variables that are also relevant for developing countries. Here, the attempt is to explain foreign direct investment flows into less developed countries.

Unstructured amalgamation of economics and politics (C)

The studies dealt with through this approach try to capture the influence of economics and politics on foreign direct investment by specifying appropriate variables. Another possibility is to introduce the investment climate in a host country by using the *country risk indicators* that have been developed by various institutions. It is tempting to relate these risk indicators directly to foreign direct investment flows. In principle, there is no need to introduce additional economic or political factors because the risk indicators claim to fulfil this task adequately.

No such economic studies presently exist with the exception of the one by Dunning discussed above, who uses the BERI but does not find any significant influence. This may be due to the fact that he simultaneously includes a great many other economic and political factors in the regression, which (at least in part) pick up similar influences on foreign direct investment behaviour.

EVALUATION OF EXISTING STUDIES

The above short discussion of some representative recent contributions to the empirical analysis of foreign direct investment shows that there is no clear picture of what factors are the main determinants. In particular, it is unknown what role the economic factors, and what role the political factors play.

The unsatisfactory state of research relates both to matters of content and to statistical methodology. With respect to content, the studies reveal a very large variance of economic and especially political factors which are introduced as prospective determinants. The studies rarely give any convincing reasons, based on theoretical notions, of why a particular variable is included and why another one is excluded. It is also quite obvious that some of the empirical results are 'explained' *ex post*; in other words, no serious effort is made to subject theoretical hypotheses to tests. A general shortcoming of the studies surveyed, therefore, is that the empirical estimation and the variables used as causal factors are not guided by theoretical considerations but are introduced *ad hoc*. The statistical procedures used in the studies on the determinants of foreign direct investment are also unsatisfactory. In many cases they are unnecessarily complicated and difficult to interpret.

These deficiencies may be overcome by (1) formulating testable hypotheses on the basis of existing theories of international production; (2) testing them by as simple a method as possible, i.e. by the multiple regression technique current in economics; and (3) emphasizing the simultaneous influence of economic and political factors. In order to do this, competing models based on approaches A, B and C above are constructed and contrasted with a politico-economic approach (approach D). The performance of the competing models will be evaluated on the basis of the model's forecasting capacity.

A POLITICO-ECONOMIC MODEL OF FOREIGN DIRECT INVESTMENT (D)

The decision of an enterprise in an industrialized country to invest directly in a developing country is motivated by a higher expected (future) profitability as compared with alternative investment possibilities at home or in other industrialized countries. But the relative advantage of such investment depends on both economic and political influences. Even if present economic conditions seem satisfactory and suggest good prospects for the future, it is quite possible that they will not materialize owing to unfavourable political conditions. It is therefore necessary to consider simultaneously the economic and political determinants of foreign investment decisions.

The theory underlying the economic determinants of foreign direct investment in developing countries allows us to formulate six testable hypotheses. The first three refer to internal economic conditions in the host country.

1 The higher the GNP per capita, the better is the nation's economic health, and the better are the prospects that direct investment will be profitable. A positive influence on foreign direct investment is expected.
2 A high rate of growth of GNP is an indicator of a good development potential in the future. This suggests a positive influence on direct investment from abroad.
3 A high rate of inflation is a sign of internal economic tension and of an inability or unwillingness of the government and the central bank to balance the budget and restrict money supply. As a rule, the higher the rate of inflation, the less inclined are foreign decision-makers to invest directly in the country. A negative relationship is hypothesized.

The next hypothesis relates to the external economic conditions of the host country.

4 A large deficit in the balance of payments indicates that the country lives beyond its means. There is an increasing danger that free capital movement will be restricted and that it will be more difficult to transfer the profits from the direct investments

into the investing country. With a deficit in the balance of payments being measured positively and a surplus negatively, the testable hypothesis is that there is a negative effect on the inflow of foreign direct investment.

The two final economic hypotheses deal with the relative advantage the labour market offers compared with alternative investment opportunities.

5 The lower the wage costs are, the more profitable it is to invest directly in the country concerned. A negative relationship to the foreign direct investment flow is hypothesized.
6 For direct investment to be worthwhile, a skilled work-force is needed. It is hypothesized that the larger the share of an age group with secondary education, *ceteris paribus*, the more direct investment will flow in. A positive relationship is hypothesized.

The theory underlying the political determinants of foreign direct investment is less well developed. Most studies consider one or two political variables only; they therefore give influences from politics little chance to affect direct investment from industrialized countries. Here, four testable hypotheses will be advanced.

7 Political instability may disrupt the economic process and affect a particular foreign investment. Internal political troubles may be projected outwards and create additional difficulties for foreign-owned firms, including the threat of partial or total nationalization. This danger exists quite irrespective of whether the government is of left-wing or right-wing persuasion, because both types may resort to nationalism to strengthen their position. It is hypothesized that increased political instability induces marginal decision-makers to undertake less direct investment. A negative relationship is expected.
8 The more left-wing the host government's ideology is, the more likely it will be that the foreign direct investor will run into trouble, *ceteris paribus*. The international direct investors are likely to perceive this danger to be lower in the case of a government with a more right-wing orientation, especially as

its rhetoric is more friendly to foreign investors. using the dummy variable 1 for right-wing and 0 for left-wing governments, a positive relationship to foreign direct investment is expected.

The following two political hypotheses take aid as an indicator of the closeness of relationships with the Communist and with the Western blocs of countries. Neither of the blocs grants aid for purely altruistic reasons; rather, evidence suggests that they do it to influence the recipient countries' political position. The amount of aid per capita may therefore also be taken as an indicator of the host countries' dependence on either the Communist or the Western bloc.

9   The larger the per capita amount of aid received by a country from the Communist bloc, the less will foreign direct investors be inclined to invest in the country. A negative relationship is hypothesized.

10 Conversely, a large amount of aid from Western countries is conducive to more foreign direct investment. A positive relationship is expected.

A final hypothesis belongs to neither the economic nor the political realm, but contains elements of both.

11 The host country's economic and political position may be eased by multilateral aid. Such aid serves to release some of the balance of payments pressure. It is given on the basis of often quite stringent restrictions by the international institutions (especially the International Monetary Fund). The international direct investors may therefore expect from the host country a more friendly political posture, and may have less fear of nationalization and curtailments of the movement of capital. A positive relationship between the amount of multilateral aid and foreign direct investment is expected.

COMPETING MODELS AND EMPIRICAL ESTIMATION

Four models will be compared with each other: models A, B and C, described on pp. 72–5 and the politico-economic model D just developed. The 'political' model A and the 'economic' model B can be taken as special cases of the more general politico-economic model D.

'Political' model A

This model is essentially confined to testing the influence of political instability on foreign direct investment flows, controlling for per capita GNP. It thus consists of hypotheses 7 and 1.

'Economic' model B

This model contains the economic determinants of model D, namely hypotheses 1–6.

'Amalgamated' model C

This model uses the Institutional Investor's Credit Rating indicator, composed of both economic and political factors. Therefore no other determinants are introduced to avoid measuring the same influence twice. Only the per capita level of GNP is controlled for (hypothesis 1).

'Politico-economic' model D

This model consists of the full set of hypotheses 1–11.

These four models have been tested econometrically by multiple regression over 54 developing countries (Frey and Schneider 1983). Table 4.5 shows the results for the year 1979.

A comparison of the four models indicates that the 'politico-economic' model D statistically explains by far the largest part of the variance, 69 per cent. The 'political' model accounts for 38 per cent, the 'economic' model for 56 per cent and the amalgamated model for 47 per cent of the variance. Most of the coefficients of all four models are statistically significant at the 95 and the 99 per cent levels of security. All the coefficients have the theoretically expected sign; the hypotheses developed need not be rejected. (The only exception is hypothesis 8, that governments with a left-wing ideology, *ceterius paribus*, deter

TABLE 4.5   Political and economic determinants of net foreign direct investment per capita, 1979: comparison of four competing models, 54 less developed countries*

Model (hypothesis)	Const.	Economic determinants					
		Real GNP per cap. (1)	Growth of real GNP (2)	Rate of infla- tion (3)	Bal. of payments deficit (4)	Wage cost (5)	Skilled work- force (6)
'Political' (A)	2.74	0.07** (4.10) [0.50]	—	—	—	—	—
'Economic' (B)	18.08	0.07** (3.11) [0.55]	4.36* (2.63) [0.27]	−0.85* (−2.24) [−0.14]	−0.29** (−4.84) [−0.54]	−0.51* (−2.31) [−0.11]	0.64* (2.02) [0.08]
'Amalgam.' (C)	3.57	0.06** (4.00) [0.49]	—	—	—	—	—
'Politico- economic' (D)	22.47	0.07** (3.02) [0.53]	3.84* (2.34) [0.21]	−0.86* (−2.29) [−0.14]	−0.26** (−4.21) [−0.51]	−0.48* (−2.11) [−0.09]	0.51 (1.84) [0.06]

* The figures in parentheses are the *t*-values. Coefficients statistically significant on the 95% level are indicated by an asterisk; on the 99% level by two asterisks. The figures in square brackets are the

direct foreign investment. The respective parameter of the politico-economic model D is statistically insignificant but has the theoretically expected sign.)

Comparing across the models, it may be noted that the sizes of the coefficients of the determinants are quite similar. This suggests that the addition of economic determinants to the 'political' model A, and the addition of political determinants to the 'economic' model B, add an independent new dimension to the estimation. As models A and B are special (extreme) cases of the 'politico-economic' model D, it indicates that the joint and simultaneous consideration of economic and political determinants as in model D is appropriate. Considering the standardized regression coefficients (β-coefficients), it may be seen that real per capita GNP is the dominating influence on foreign direct invest-

	Political determinants				Political and economic multi-lateral aid (11)	Test-statistics			Degrees of freedom
Instit. invest. credit rating	Polit. insta-bility (7)	Govt. ideology (right = 1 left = 0) (8)	Bilateral aid received: from Communist countries (9)	from Western countries (10)		$\bar{R}^2$	Stand. error	$\hat{F}$	
—	−0.43* (−2.59) [−0.13]	—	—	—	—	0.38	39.94	8.81	52
—	—	—	—	—	—	0.56	28.41	12.47	47
0.15** (2.89) [0.34]	—	—	—	—	—	0.47	31.43	10.47	52
—	−0.36* (−2.27) [−0.11]	2.43 (1.43) [0.06]	−0.49* (−2.57) [−0.11]	0.96** (4.39) [0.56]	0.35* (2.41) [0.11]	0.69	20.41	23.56	42

standardized β regression coefficients.
Source: Frey and Schneider (1983).

ment flows in all three models. The only determinant with a higher (absolute) β-coefficient suggests that bilateral aid from Western countries – an influence that is taken into account in the politico-economic model D only – is of great importance. The only other factor with a high β-coefficient is the balance of payments deficit (models B and D).

COMPARISON OF FORECASTING PERFORMANCE

The previous section has shown that all four models are quite satisfactory, judged from the point of view of the usual test statistics. The politico-economic model, which combines economic and political determinants, performs relatively the best with respect to goodness of fit ($\bar{R}^2$).

A more demanding and therefore more relevant test is a model's forecasting capacity. The four competing models were analysed to determine which is best able to predict foreign direct investment on the basis of the estimation equation for 1979. For that purpose, the true values of the independent variables for 1980 are used for comparison (*ex post* prediction). The results are presented in table 4.6 This table indicates that the average absolute and percentage deviation of the econometric prediction from the true value is smallest for the politico-economic model D, followed by the economic model B. The worst *ex post* predictions are by the political model A. On average, the politico-economic

TABLE 4.6   Forecasting performance of four competing models to explain foreign direct investment: *ex post* forecasts for 1980 on the basis of estimates for 1979

	Model			
				'Politico-
	'Political'	*'Economic'*	*'Amalgamated'*	*economic'*
	(A)	*(B)*	*(C)*	*(D)*
Average absolute residual ($)	28.8	17.9	34.4	11.6
Percentage deviation from the true value	56.9%	35.4%	48.2%	23.0%

Source: Frey and Schneider (1983).

model D has an absolute prediction error of per capita foreign direct investment of $12 or 23 per cent, while the second-best model – the purely economic model B – has an error of $18 or 35 per cent, a quite sizeable difference.

It may be concluded that foreign direct investment in developing countries is determined simultaneously by both economic and political factors. It may further be concluded that an amalgamation of economic and political influences into a credit risk indicator is not advisable because it is not able to do justice to the complexity of politico-economic interdependence.

The most important economic determinants seem to be a

country's level of development (as measured by real per capita GNP) and the state of its balance of payments. The higher the per capita income and the lower the balance of payments deficit, the more foreign direct investment is attracted. Among the less important economic influences are the growth of GNP and the workers' skill level, attracting foreign direct investment, and inflation and wage costs, reducing the inflow of foreign direct investment.

Among the political determinants, the amount of bilateral aid coming from Western countries has the strongest stimulating effect. When a host country receives aid from Communist countries this has a significantly negative, but not such an important, effect. Multilateral aid also significantly furthers foreign direct investment. Another relevant factor is political instability, which significantly reduces the inflow of foreign direct investment; while the government's ideological position (right- or left-wing orientation) does not have a statistically significant influence.

CONCLUSION

There is much concern at present about the risk involved in international lending as well as in foreign direct investment. Such investments are subject to a great variety of risks that do not arise when investments are undertaken within one's own country. The most obvious country risk is expropriation or forced divestment. Empirical studies suggest, however, that this risk is not very high, and that it differs considerably between the sectors invested in. Country risk is informally assessed by relying on expert opinion or by a quantitative analysis of past data.

Foreign direct investment is influenced by a multitude of determinants, but most studies consider either political or economic factors only. To overcome this shortcoming, four models are developed with the purpose of comparing the quality of the estimates and (ex post) forecasts: a model that concentrates exclusively on a political determinant (political instability); a model that concentrates exclusively on economic determinants (growth of GNP, inflation, balance of payments, wage costs, skilled labour force); and a model that uses as the sole determinant an international risk indicator, an amalgamation of economic and political factors are compared with a politico-economic model, which simultaneously includes both economic and political determinants. The political variables of government ideology and the type of bilateral, as well as multilateral, aid are also included among the explanatory variables. It turns out that, with respect to both the goodness of fit and the quality of (*ex post*) forecasts, the politico-economic model performs significantly better than the three other models.

FURTHER READING

WORKS MENTIONED IN THE TEXT

Agarwal, Jamuna P. (1980), 'Determinants of Foreign Direct Investment: A Survey'. *Weltwirtschaftliches Archiv*, 116, 739–73.

Dunning, John H. (1981), 'Explaining the International Direct Investment Position of Countries: Towards a Dynamic or Developmental Approach'. *Weltwirtschaftliches Archiv*, 117, 30–64.

Frey, Bruno S. and Schneider, Friedrich (1983), 'Economic and Political Determinants of Foreign Direct Investment'. Institute for Empirical Economic Research, University of Zurich, mimeo.

Green, Robert T. (1972), *Political Instability as a Determinant of US Foreign Investment*. Austin, Texas: Bureau of Business Research, University of Texas.

Group of Thirty (1982), *Risks in International Bank Lending*. New York: Group of Thirty.

Kobrin, Stephen J. (1976), 'The Environmental Determinants of Foreign Direct Manufacturing Investment: An Ex-Post Empirical Analysis'. *Journal of International Business Studies*, 7, 29–42.

Kobrin, Stephen J. (1980), 'Foreign Enterprise and Forced Divestment in LDCs'. *International Organization*, 34 (Winter), 65–88.

Kobrin, Stephen J. (1982), *Managing Political Risk Assessment*. Berkeley. University of California Press.

Kudrle, Robert T. and Bobrow, Davis B. (1982), 'US Policy toward Foreign Direct Investment'. *World Politics*, 34 (April), 353–79.

Levis, Mario (1979), 'Does Political Instability in Developing Countries Affect Foreign Investment Flow? An Empirical Examination'. *Management International Review*, 19, 59–68.

Rummel, R. J. and Heenan, David A. (1978), 'How Multinationals Analyze Political Risk'. *Harvard Business Review*, 56, 67–76.

Thunell, Lars H. (1977), *Political Risks in International Business. Investment Behavior of Multinational Corporations*. New York: Praeger.

UN Centre on Transnational Corporations (1983), *Salient Features and Trends in Foreign Direct Investment*. New York: United Nations.

Williams, M. L. (1975), 'The Extent and Significance of the Nationalization of Foreign-owned Assets in Developing Countries, 1956–1972'. *Oxford Economic Papers*, 27, 260–73.

WORKS RELATING TO FURTHER ASPECTS DISCUSSED

A general discussion of the various problems associated with country risk is given in

Herring, Richard J. (ed.) (1983), *Managing International Risk*. Cambridge: Cambridge University Press.

Basic literature on multinational firms that are most involved in foreign direct investment is

Dunning, John H. (ed.) (1974), *Economic Analysis and the Multinational Enterprise*. London: Allen and Unwin.

Kindleberger, Charles P. and Andretsch, David B. (eds) (1983), *The Multinational Corporation in the 1980s*. Cambridge, Mass.: MIT Press.

An econometric study of foreign direct investment in developed economies is

Scaperlanda, Anthony, and Balough, Robert S. (1983), 'Determinants of US Direct Investment in the EEC'. *European Economic Review*, 21, 381–90.

5

Who Gives and Receives Foreign Aid?

In 1981 the absolute net aid disbursements by governments, or *official* development assistance, amounted to roughly $35 billion. More than 70 per cent of this official aid came from the industrialized countries, the rest mainly from OPEC members, while the countries of the Soviet bloc extended very little aid. The countries of the Development Assistance Committee within the Organization for Economic Co-operation and Development (OECD) agreed to spend 0.7 per cent of their respective GNPs on official aid. The target has already been overshot in 1980/81 by the Netherlands, with 1.05 per cent of GNP, and Norway, Sweden and Denmark, with over 0.75 per cent of GNP. Other countries, such as the Federal Republic of Germany and Canada (around 0.45 per cent of GNP), and the United Kingdom (roughly 0.4 per cent of GNP), are far from meeting the target. The United States lags far behind; it spends only 0.25 per cent of GNP on official development assistance (see OECD 1982, pp. 61–4).

AID IS NOT ONLY PHILANTHROPIC

Everyone knows that the economic aid given by the governments of industrialized countries to less developed countries is scarcely given for philanthropic and humanitarian reasons. The donor countries act from selfish motives, expecting an economic and/or political benefit from such action. It is also well known that some LDCs manage to get much aid, and from different sources, while other nations are less successful.

The donor nations may have various economic motives for helping poorer countries. Aid may be expected to stimulate additional exports of the donor country; it may help to get rid of burdensome surpluses, especially of agricultural products; it may contribute to an increase in the production of raw materials that the donor country wants to import (at a reasonable price); and it may help to improve the climate for successful foreign direct investments in the aid-receiving country.

Foreign aid to developing countries may also yield various types of political pay-offs – for example an increase in influence on the political and cultural decisions relevant to the donor country; a strengthening of the position of the government or regime in power, with which the donor country has friendly relationships; an improvement of the military security of the donor state by fostering an ally; and a rise in international prestige by projecting the image of a humanitarian country.

These and other justifications for giving aid to countries of the Third World are, on the whole, in the interest of the donor country concerned. The question is: Which actors within a country have a motivation to act in the nation's interest? Are there any incentives for the voters, interest groups or government to act on behalf of the nation's foreign interests? To answer these questions it is necessary to look at the role of international aid within the political economy of the donor country.

AID IN DOMESTIC POLITICS

The self-interest model of public choice (pp. 5–7) may again be applied to the actors' behaviour with respect to international aid-giving. Voters are not very interested in the amount of aid going to foreign countries because they derive, at best, an indirect and non-monetary benefit from it, and they therefore make little effort to become well-informed on the particular issues involved. Nevertheless, their general feelings about foreign aid in the form of an undifferentiated 'public opinion' have some impact on the foreign aid decision-making process. Some interest groups (e.g. exporters) will push for more aid in order to reap economic benefits, while others (e.g. churches or the Red Cross) will advocate aid for purely humanitarian reasons. However, such interests are few and weakly organized, compared with industrial pressure groups such as trade unions or producers' organizations. In particular, they have much smaller financial resources available to make their case in the political arena.

The government is able to use the discretionary room provided by voters and interest groups to further its own goals. International aid is especially useful in promoting a desired foreign policy. A country's 'international standing' may be an important issue for members of a government; they will derive high benefits in terms of prestige, and possibly influence, if the nation they represent enjoys high esteem internationally. Moreover, owing to the discretionary room left to them by voters and interest groups, politicians have a chance to put into effect their ideological notions about what a 'good' policy is – a possibility that they rarely have with respect to domestic economic policy.

It is not unlikely that the politicians will fill this discretionary space by pursuing an aid-giving policy that is in line with the 'country's' interests as discussed above. The public officials representing a country externally (the diplomats and the many public officials involved in the host of international negotiations) also have an interest in seeing their country in good standing internationally, and will tend to support the politicians in their aid-giving policy. In an international setting a government will tend to speak out for international aid, but it will be careful not to make any firm commitments: one can aptly speak of a 'rhetoric of aid' (Wall 1973). However, when financial decisions have to be made that affect the domestic economy, the government will be rather more reluctant to grant a large amount of international aid because it will usually stand to benefit more by allocating the funds to groups within the country.

THE ADVANTAGE OF NON-COMMITMENT

The recipient countries may actively influence the amount of aid given to them by donor countries who are interested in their support in the international sphere. A country is likely to receive little aid if it *always* supports the donor country politically, or if it *never* supports the donor country. It can expect to get the highest amount of aid if it makes it clear that the political position it takes will depend upon the amount of aid received. Thus, a country wishing to maximize the amount of foreign aid it receives should not be a permanent member of any international bloc but rather should make it clear that its political position *can* be influenced by the giving of more aid.

This situation may be formalized with the help of game theory. A given coalition of countries (one or several donor nations and LDCs receiving aid from them) that form an economic or political alliance (such as the European Community or NATO) may have the 'power' to achieve certain economic and/or political aims. When an LDC joins such a coalition, this power may increase. The LDC considered thus has 'power' in the sense of being able to affect the coalition's achievements. A country that is *always* aligned with the coalition is in this sense 'powerless'; it is of little interest to a donor country that wants to increase the influence of its coalition. The clearest case obtains when a coalition of countries will achieve a benefit if they have the majority of the votes in an assembly or organization, but no benefit if they have a minority. The decisive member of the coalition is that country which may turn a minority into a majority. In that particular case, power is attributed to a country that is in the median position between the countries belonging to the coalitions.

The concept of 'power' used in game theory, though well defined, is not easily identifiable in reality. Moreover, the concept relates to only one particular aspect of the relationships of donor and recipient countries with respect to international aid. The model should not therefore be taken to give a complete picture of aid-giving. However, it is well suited to draw our attention to the fact that international aid is not a unilateral action going from developed to less developed countries, but rather the result of interdependent activities in which the recipient countries have their say.

INTERACTION BETWEEN COMPETING DONORS AND RECIPIENTS

An industrialized country giving aid to a less developed country rarely does so unconditionally, but rather on the premise that the recipient country will take a political position favourable to the donor country, measured for instance by the proportion of votes it casts in line with the donor country's wishes in the United Nations. As a rule, the donor country will be willing to invest more aid to a particular country, the higher the return in terms of support that it receives from the country getting aid. A Third World country, call it Thirdonia, may aspire to receive aid simultaneously from various donor countries, say from Usonia and Russonia, by taking some intermediate position between these two super-powers. Depending on the reaction of the two donor countries, the total amount of aid received by Thirdonia will rise or fall as it moves away from total commitment to one power towards a neutralist position in the middle. Figure 5.1 shows the amount of aid received (vertical axis) when positions on the alignment scale (horizontal axes) are occupied by Thirdonia. In figure 5.1(a) aid to Thirdonia from Usonia falls only little as it moves towards a neutralist middle ground, and the same applies when it moves away from Russonia's position. This behaviour of the donor countries results in total aid (top line) increasing. Figure 5.1(b) shows the case in which each of the donor countries cuts aid strongly when Thirdonia moves away from its own position, which results in a decline of total aid received when Thirdonia is non-aligned. The total aid curves

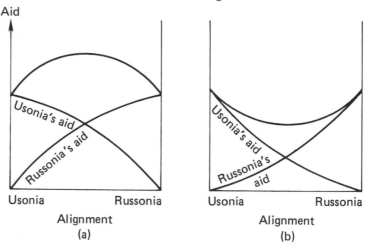

FIGURE 5.1 Types of donor country reaction to recipient country alignment positions: (a) 'non-penalizing neutralism (NPN); (b) 'penalizing neutralism' (PN).

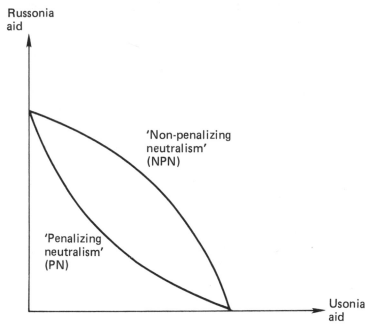

FIGURE 5.2 Opportunity sets of aid-receiving country.

shown in the figure determine the aid *opportunity set* available to Thirdonia upon choosing alignment positions (see figure 5.2).

The reactions of Usonia's and Russonia's 'non-penalizing neutralism' (NPN), shown in figure 5.1(a), result in a traditionally shaped (convex) opportunity set; while an insistence on alignment on the part of the aid-givers, or 'penalizing neutralism' (PN), as depicted in figure 5.1(b), results in a transformation curve bent towards the origin.

The model (Hirschman 1964) is closed by making two alternative assumptions about the preference function of the aid-receiving country. If it is interested only in maximizing total aid received, irrespective of the source, the preference indifference map consists of straight lines such as AM (for 'aid maximization'). This is shown in figure 5.3. If however Thirdonia puts high utility on having an independent position (i.e. if its marginal utility diminishes when it relies increasingly on one donor country only), its indifference curves will have the traditional shape, such as NA (for 'non-alignment').

The total amount of aid received by Thirdonia and the contributions to it by Usonia and Russonia, as well as the alignment position of the recipient country, may be determined by joining Thirdonia's opportunity set (figure 5.2) and its indifference curves (figure 5.3).

Consider first the case in which the Third World country has a preference for *non alignment*. A stable equilibrium is achieved when the two donor countries act in a way that does not penalize neutralism (NPN, in figure 5.1(a)). Figure 5.4 shows that Thirdonia reaches its highest utility level at point E, receiving aid a_R from Russonia and a_U from Usonia, in total $a_R + a_U$. If, however, the donor countries react differently to a deflection from their own position and punish neutralism (PN in figure 5.1(b)), then it is possible that corner solutions will be the outcome. Thirdonia will switch its position to total commitment to either Russonia or Usonia.

If Thirdonia is an *aid-maximizing* country, not considering

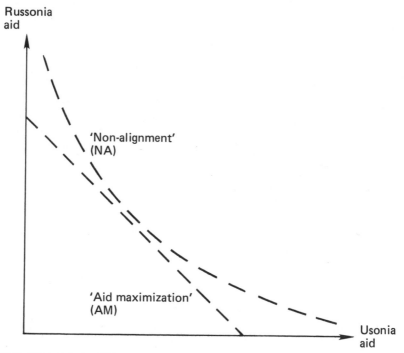

FIGURE 5.3 Indifference curves of aid-receiving country.

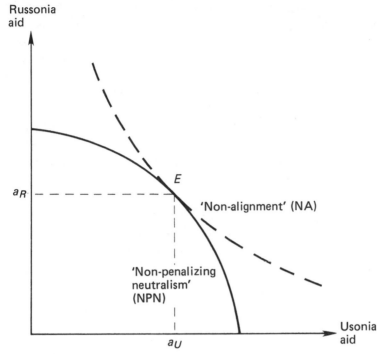

FIGURE 5.4 Stable equilibrium of aid distribution.

independence as having a value of its own with a straight-line indifference curve (see figure 5.3), its optimum policy is again to take such a position that both Russonia and Usonia supply aid, provided they do not punish neutralism. The equilibrium is of the same type as in figure 5.4.

However, when the donor countries punish any deviation from their allegiance by strongly reducing aid (PN behaviour), the effect will always be that Thirdonia will side completely with either Russonia or Usonia (see figure 5.5). A position at point P yields Thirdonia more utility than one at point P', i.e., it fares better by siding completely with Usonia, receiving no aid from Russonia.

However, if Russonia decides to increase the aid it offers in return for total commitment (say from point P' to P''), Thirdonia will switch sides completely and accept aid only from Russonia, raising its utility AM_2 ($> AM_1$).

It should be noted that such an increase in aid by one country does not have this effect when donor countries do not penalize neutralism. As may be seen from figure 5.4, a similar outward shift of the NPN opportunity set in the upward direction (more Russonia aid, given Usonia aid) would not lead to a complete change in alignment. Thirdonia's policy of switching sides completely is thus due to the donor's strong punishment of neutralist behaviour.

This highly abstract model is able to deal with total aid, the distribution of aid between donors and the alignment of the aid-receiving country. It may easily be extended, for instance by considering the fact that the donor's behaviour may not be symmetric, as has been assumed so far. Thus, Usonia may be prepared not to punish neutralism, while Russonia may reduce aid strongly if a country defects, as shown in figure 5.6. Under

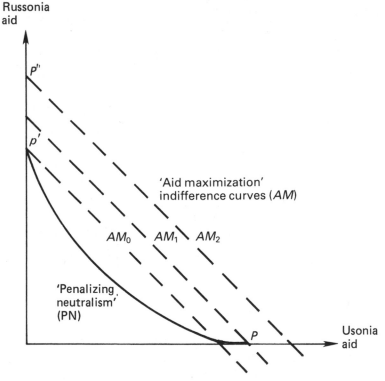

FIGURE 5.5 Total commitment of Thirdonia to either Usonia or Russonia.

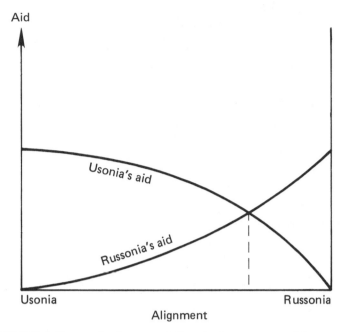

FIGURE 5.6 Russonia does, and Usonia does not, punish neutralism.

these circumstances it may no longer be known *a priori* whether a neutralist position of Thirdonia will lead to more or less aid; the relative amount of aid received then no longer indicates Thirdonia's alignment. As may be seen in the figure, when Thirdonia takes *equal* amounts of aid from both donors, it is more closely associated with Russonia.

This model is useful from two points of view. First, it shows that, when aid-giving is the result of an effort to yield political influence, an interaction of behaviour between the donor and the recipient countries emerges. The general result of the game-theoretic model of the previous section is confirmed: if the aid-receiving country (or countries) has a possibility of influencing the outcome, it is not 'powerless'. The model also shows that the interaction is quite complex and that the behaviour of each actor has to be identified before any conclusions can be drawn.

Second, the model shows how the tools of economic analysis – here, transformation and indifference curves – can be applied to analyse important aspects of international political economics. It shows once again that economic thinking can be usefully applied also to study politico-economic interactions.

IS AID AN INTERNATIONAL PUBLIC GOOD?

A government of a country, and especially its inhabitants, may derive utility not only from giving aid itself, but also from the recipient country's receiving aid from other countries. What matters in this case is not so much the donor country's own contribution to the developing country (i.e., its own input) but rather the *total* aid received by that country, irrespective of who contributes it. On the other hand, if aid is a means of influencing the recipient country, the government (and population) of the particular country considered may experience a utility loss when other countries extend such aid.

These relationships may usefully be analysed in the context of a simple model (Dudley 1979). Taking U as the utility derived from giving aid, A as the amount of aid given by the government of a particular country, and A^o the aid given by other countries, one may define

$$U = A + \alpha A^o$$

If $\alpha = 0$, the government's and population's utility is unaffected by the aid given by other countries. Should $\alpha > 0$, however, the government and population of the country considered will benefit not only form their own country's aid disbursement, but also from that of other countries. Aid confers positive spill-overs beyond national boundaries and may be considered an international public good. In the special case in which $\alpha = 1$, or $U = A + A^o$, the donor makes no distinction between his own spending and that of other countries.In that case aid is a *pure* international public good characterized by non-rivalry and non-excludability between nations.

It may also be possible that $\alpha < 0$: the utility of the government and population of the donor country may increase when its own aid increases and fall when the aid is given by another country. As argued above, this utility loss may be due to the fact that the donor in question fears that the other countries will exert unwelcome influence on the recipient country.

Depending on which of the three cases ($\alpha = 0$, $\alpha > 0$, $\alpha < 0$) obtains, the donor countries will extend different amounts of aid. Assume for simplicity that each donor determines its aid disbursement taking the aid from others as given. In order to make the amount of aid comparable, assume further that there are two donor countries with equal per capita incomes, but that one has a small and the other a large population. When the behaviour of the two countries is independent, there being no utility interaction ($\alpha = 0$), aid per capita A/N will be equal for the small and the large country ($A_s/N_s = A_L/N_L$).

A possible combination of aid disbursement is indicated by $P_{\alpha = 0}$ in figure 5.7. With aid as an international public good ($\alpha > 0$), the small country reacts to the (given) aid spending of the large country. The reaction curve R_sR_s depicted in figure 5.7 has a *negative* slope: the greater the aid given by the large country A_L, the less aid is given by the small country A_S, since its government and population also derive utility from the large country's aid-giving. This substitution effect also holds for the large country, so that its reaction curve R_LR_L also has a negative slope. The two reaction curves intersect at point $P_{\alpha > 0}$. There,

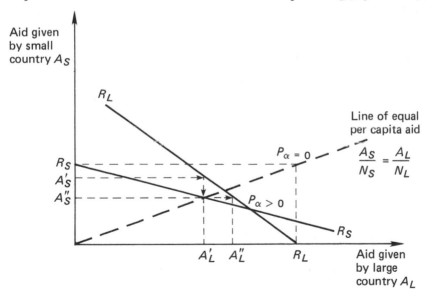

FIGURE 5.7 Equilibrium between countries with aid as an international public good ($\alpha>0$).

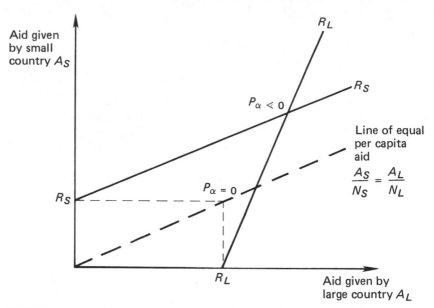

FIGURE 5.8 Equilibrium between countries when another country's aid is resented ($\alpha<0$).

the two countries are in equilibrium; neither has an incentive to change its aid disbursement. This equilibrium is stable; if the countries start off with a different amount of aid, they will converge on $P_{\alpha > 0}$.

Assume for example that the small country allocates A'_S to aid. The large country then decides to give aid A'_L. This in turn motivates the small country to reduce its aid (because it derives utility from the large country's aid) and it will give A''_S. The large country then increases its aid to A''_L; etc. It is easy to see that the aid allocations approach the equilibrium point $P_{\alpha > 0}$. Each country spends *less* than it would if it were acting in isolation ($\alpha = 0$): compare point $P_{\alpha = 0}$ with $P_{\alpha > 0}$ in figure 5.7. It may also be seen that the equilibrium is below the equal per capita aid line. Not surprisingly, the small country spends less aid per capita than the large country; it tends to act as a free-rider on international aid.

What happens when a country is negatively affected by the other country's aid ($\alpha < 0$)? In this case the two reaction curves have a *positive* slope, as shown in figure 5.8. The (stable) equilibrium $P_{\alpha\,<\,0}$ now lies above and to the right of the equal per capita aid line: each country spends more on aid than if it were acting in isolation (indicated by $P_{\alpha\,=\,0}$), and the small country contributes more aid per capita than the large country.

The model has been empirically tested to determine whether foreign aid can be considered an international public good ($\alpha > 0$) or whether the negative effects of other countries' aid prevail ($\alpha < 0$). The following 'aid demand function' has been estimated from data for the 17 members of the Development Assistance Committee of OECD over a three-year average for the years 1972–4:

$$\frac{A_i}{N_i} = \delta_0 + \delta_1\bar{y} + \delta_2\frac{A^o}{N_i} + \delta_3\frac{1}{N_i}$$

Net official bilateral or multilateral per capita development assistance A_i/N_i given by a donor i is explained by the per capita GNP of a donor country $\bar{y}$, by the net official development assistance given by other donors in the donor's reference group (standardized by the population of donor i) A^o/N_i and by the reciprocal of i's population $1/N_i$. Four reference groups are distinguished: the European Economic Community, the European Free Trade Association, North America, and Oceania (comprising Australia and New Zealand). The result of the estimation of the parameters δ_0, δ_1, δ_2 and δ_3 is shown in table 5.1.

It may be seen that the equation is able to account for 55 per cent of the variation in bilateral aid, and for 43 per cent in the case of multilateral aid. The higher the per capita income of the donor, the more is spent, both bilaterally and multilaterally, on aid. The per capita aid of other countries in a donor's reference group also has a statistically significant effect on aid disbursements: it turns out that a country's per capita aid is the larger, the more is spent by the other countries.

The empirical estimate thus suggests that international aid is *not* a public good from which all nations benefit. Indeed, it may be shown that $\delta_2 = -\alpha/(1 + c)$ (where c is a positive constant): as the estimated value of δ_2 is larger than zero in the estimate, it follows that $\alpha < 0$. This indicates that the donor countries analysed resent the aid being given by other countries, and that they tend to increase their own aid-spending when other coun-

TABLE 5.1   Determinants of foreign aid to developing countries by 17 industrialized countries, 1972–4*

Determining variable		Coefficients Bilateral aid	Multilateral aid
Constant	δ_0	−3.86	−3.09
Per capita income of donor	δ_1	0.003**	0.002*
		(3.60)	(2.42)
Per capita aid of other countries in reference group	δ_2	0.02*	0.04*
		(2.29)	(2.21)
Reciprocal of size of population of donor	δ_3	−14.1	5.22
		(−1.70)	(0.82)
	$\bar{R}^2$	54.5%	43.3%

*The model is estimated by a simultaneous estimation procedure (two-stage least-square) because A_i depends on A^0, and A^0 depends on A_i, provided $\delta_2 = 0$. The numbers in parantheses are the t-values.

Source: Dudley (1979), table 3 (selected figures).

tries do in order to maintain their influence in the international arena. (Another possible interpretation of the finding is that the foreign aid agencies find it easier to get their budget increases approved if they are able to point to large aid budgets in other donor countries.)

Accordingly, figure 5.8 seems to be more realistic than figure 5.7. The positive reaction to each other's aid among the donors is to the benefit of the developing countries. As the analysis of figure 5.8 shows, total aid, and aid by each donor, is larger than it would be if aid were given in isolation ($\alpha = 0$), or if aid were an international public good ($\alpha > 0$).

CONCLUSION

International aid is rarely given by industrialized countries to developing countries for philanthropic reasons, but rather serves the selfish motive of exercising political influence. Governments usually have considerable discretionary room in the aid-giving sphere, as voters and interest groups pay relatively little attention to that aspect of politics. Both politicians and public officials derive private benefits (in particular, prestige) from projecting a beneficial picture of their country in the international community. They therefore tend to advocate international aid but are not eager to carry the financial consequences, as it is generally more advantageous for them to spend the money for the benefit of their own voters and interest groups.

The recipient countries may influence the amount of aid they get if the donor countries are in competition with each other: they have some measure of 'power' because the donor countries are interested in receiving their political support. While the interaction between the competing donors and recipients is quite complex, it is possible to draw interesting conclusions about the amount of total aid given, its distribution between donors and the political alignment of the aid-receiving country with the help of simple tools of economic analysis.

An econometric model tested for 17 industrialized donor countries suggests that nations resent aid being given by other nations because they fear that they thereby lose influence in the international sphere. Therefore they tend to reciprocate by increasing their own aid expenditures when competing nations do so. This aid competition is to the benefit of the developing countries, who receive more aid than they would if the countries acted in isolation or if they considered aid to be an international public good.

FURTHER READING

WORKS MENTIONED IN THE TEXT

Dudley, Leonard (1979), 'Foreign Aid and the Theory of Alliances'. *Review of Economics and Statistics*, 61 (November), 564–71.

Hirschman, Albert O. (1964), 'The Stability of Neutralism: A Geometrical Note'. *American Economic Review*, 54 (March), 94–100; reprinted in Bruce M. Russett (ed.), *Economic Theories of International Politics*. Chicago: Markham, 1964.

OECD (1982), *Development Co-operation: 1982 Review*. Paris: OECD.

Wall, David (1973), *The Charity of Nations. The Political Economy of Foreign Aid*. New York: Basic Books.

WORKS RELATING TO FURTHER ASPECTS DISCUSSED

For the motives for foreign aid see

Little, I. M. D. and Clifford, J. M. (1965), *International Aid*. Chicago: Aldine.

McNeil, Desmond (1981), *The Contradictions of Foreign Aid*. London: Croom Helm.

Mikesell, Raymond F. (1968), *The Economics of Foreign Aid*. London: Weidenfeld & Nicolson.

The game-theoretic model is based on the idea of the 'pivotal' voter changing a non-winning into a winning coalition. The concept is well discussed in

Luce, Duncan and Raiffa, Howard (1967), *Games and Decisions*. New York: John Wiley.

The model underlying figure 5.8 is similar to the one developed by Lewis Richardson to explain arms races:

Richardson, Lewis (1960), *Arms and Insecurity*. Pittsburgh: Bonwood Press.

6

Are Trade Wars Successful?

AN OFTEN TRIED EXERCISE

In 1956 the US government under President Eisenhower strongly opposed the intervention by Britain and France in Egypt to recover control of the Suez Canal. Fearing a devaluation of the pound, holders of sterling accounts and also the American Federal Reserve Bank started a massive conversion of English pounds into gold and other currencies. The British government thereby came under heavy monetary pressure; but the United States prevented it from drawing on its quota with the International Monetary Fund and agreed to support Britain only after its government accepted a cease-fire under the supervision of the United Nations. According to Harold Macmillan, then Chancellor of the Exchequer, the loss of reserves was *not* decisive for that decision. A sustained pressure on reserves would have led to a devaluation of the pound, but it could have been withstood for some time, and certainly much longer than the very limited period needed to have completed the military occupation of the Canal zone (Renwick 1981, p. 63).

This is an instance of applying financial pressure in order to force another country to behave in a desired way. Before and since, there have been a great many examples in which economic pressure has been used to influence a country's behaviour:

1 The Napoleonic Wars are the first instance of a large-scale 'continental blockade' (against Britain).
2 Communist China was the object of Western (particularly US) embargoes since the early 1950s, which were (partly) lifted only in the 1970s.

3 Cuba was subject to sanctions by the Organization of American States (OAS), encouraged by the United States for over a decade (1964–75).

4 The United Nations have for many years asked for economic sanctions against South Africa in order to force it to give up its racial policy and give Namibia its independence.

5 The most spectacular recent example of using trade as a weapon is that of the Arab oil-producing nations. In November 1973 the Arab oil ministers of OPEC decided to cut oil production by 25 per cent and to put a complete embargo on oil shipments to the United States and the Netherlands because of their alleged (military) support of Israel. Moreover, oil-importing nations would receive continued supplies only if they adopted a political position friendly to the Arab cause. Partly as a result of this action, the price of Persian Gulf crude oil rose from $2.30 per barrel in October 1973 to $11.65 in January 1974. Western European nations and Japan quickly responded by pledging friendship and offering bilateral agreements, arms and economic assistance to Arab nations and refusing to co-operate in the American airlift of military equipment to Israel during the October war (Doxey 1980, pp. 24–7).

6 An even more recent instance of the imposition of economic sanctions has been the refusal by the United States to supply grain to the Soviet Union after the latter invaded Afghanistan in December 1979. The European Community as well as Australia and Canada supported this decision by declaring that they would not compensate for the American reduction of exports by increasing their own exports. Argentine, on the contrary, greatly increased her exports to the Soviet Union. The embargo was ended in April 1981, mainly as a result of the American agricultural lobby, which resented having to carry the main burden of the boycott.

TYPES OF ECONOMIC SANCTIONS

There are a great many forms and techniques by which the behaviour of other nations can be influenced by subjecting them to economic pressure. As the examples provided have made clear, the most important form of economic warfare is the *boycott* or *embargo*, by which imports and/or exports of the sanctioned nation are cut.

Compared with this direct intervention into foreign trade, there may also be *financial sanctions*, such as the blocking of a nation's assets. The foreign trade embargo may relate to selected goods or to all imports and exports. Selective sanctions are not easy to operate, as serious difficulties of interpretation may arise as to what trade is permitted and what is not. Their effectiveness depends on the extent to which they are concentrated on particularly vulnerable export and import products such as special foodstuffs, weapons and advanced technology. The boycotts may be imposed gradually, by increasing the scope and intensity of sanctions over time, or immediately and in full force. A progressive application of sanctions may be less effective because it allows more time for the target economy to adapt.

Economic sanctions may be used in peacetime, usually as an alternative to military means, or in times of war as a complement to military operations. The principal purpose of economic sanctions in war is to prevent resources from falling into the hands of the enemy and to acquire as many resources as possible.

In the First World War Britain blockaded Germany as a reaction to submarine warfare; the blockade covered all goods. In the Second World War the British Ministry of Economic Warfare began to blockade German exports in November 1939, with considerable success. The main measure to prevent imports into Germany was not interception at sea but controls at the sources, in order to prevent goods destined for the enemy from being shipped at all.

In the early days of the 'phoney war' the blockade was considered Britain's main offensive weapon. The government hoped for an eventual collapse of the German 'home front' owing to the economic pressures. These calculations were soon made irrelevant by Germany's military success against France, Poland and (initially) Russia: considerable stocks and the Rumanian oil fields were captured. Only when the German armies were forced to retreat in the east did the supply position become critical. However, much was made up for by last-minute improvements in the German production of synthetic oil. According to the official

British history of economic warfare in 1939–45, 'at no stage of the war was Germany decisively weakened by shortages due to the blockade alone' (Medlicott 1952–9).

A crucial distinction is between sanctions imposed by one country or by a collectivity of nations. Collective sanctions have been used by various organizations, in particular by the League of Nations in 1935–6 against fascist Italy because of the military invasion of Ethiopia, and by the United Nations in 1966–79 against Rhodesia. When only one country blockades another one the effect is likely to be small, because the sanctioned country has many possible other countries to get its imports from and to sell its exports to. Only in very rare cases can the boycotting country prevent such substitution. For that reason, boycotting nations seek the support of other nations, and if possible all other nations.

Collective sanctions, however, are faced with another important problem. The sanctions imposed have the character of a public good for the participating nations. While each participant may agree that the country in question ought to be punished economically, each has an incentive to break the rules, and to supply the boycotted goods (at a high price) and buy the country's exports (at a good discount). Economic sanctions seem to be observed most strictly if the two forms of sanction are combined; there must be one country that vigorously pushes for the sanctions and continually sees to it that the other countries maintain the boycott, and there must be a large enough collectivity of countries participating to make substitution difficult.

CONDITIONS FOR THE SUCCESS OF ECONOMIC SANCTIONS

The theory of sanctions rests on the assumption that, if a nation is subjected to economic penalties, it will as a matter of self-interest change its conduct in the direction desired. It is therefore necessary to distinguish three conditions for the success of economic sanctions:

1 the sanctions politically decided must be actually applied (*organizational* conditions);

2 the sanctions must have the expected economic effects;
3 the economic effects must have the desired political effects.

Clearly, these conditions are hierarchical; if the organizational conditions are not met then the expected economic (and political) effects will not come about, and if there are no economic effects, the expected political effects will not materialize.

ORGANIZATIONAL CONDITIONS

In order for economic sanctions to be effective, an external and an internal precondition must obtain.

1 The embargo must be universal. No country can be allowed to form an alliance with the country boycotted, and it may not have the chance to buy and sell the goods on third markets. Countries not participating in the embargo may not compensate the export and import losses suffered by the boycotted country. This means that free-riding in the case of collective sanctions must be overcome, and that positive incentives must be created that motivate the countries to keep to the rules.
2 In order for economic sanctions to be politically maintainable within the boycotting country, the burdens (in particular the loss of exports) must be at least partly compensated for; otherwise the corresponding interest groups will lobby to end the sanctions officially or unofficially. An effective boycotting policy therefore necessitates a redistribution scheme, in order that the burdens of sanctioning are distributed in a politically acceptable way.

It goes without saying that these two preconditions for effective sanctions are rather demanding.

Furthermore, the foreign trade of a country will be boycotted effectively only if (see Hasse 1977):

1 the embargo is applied without a time lag, so that the boycotted country has no time to adjust;
2 the embargo is total or the list of goods included in a selective or 'strategic' embargo has no leaks, and is changed in an appropriate way to make effective substitution impossible;

3   there are no conflicts among the public administrations in charge of the sanctions. It must be possible to control the trade flows, which requires a complex administration having sufficient incentives to enforce the sanctions. This is particularly difficult in the case of international firms and for new products to which the list of boycotts is not (yet) adapted.

ECONOMIC CONDITIONS

Provided the blockade is based on an effective international as well as national political decision and is indeed functioning from the organizational point of view, another set of conditions has to be met in order that the sanctions will really impose economic hardship on the country boycotted. The conditions can be identified using the analysis of the gains from trade as discussed in chapter 2.

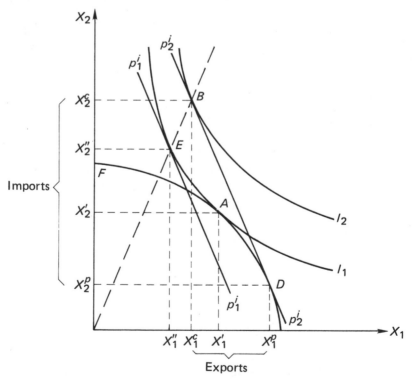

FIGURE 6.1   Real income loss arising from boycott of trade.

Figure 2.1 is reproduced for convenience here as figure 6.1. Point B shows the amounts consumed of two goods (X_1^c, X_2^c) and D indicates the amounts produced (X_1^p, X_2^p). The goods are internationally traded at the prices reigning in the international market (indicated by the slope of the price line, $p_2^i p_2^i$)   This line also indicates the real income associated with the welfare level, I_2. If the country is cut off from international trade, it has to consume and produce at point A, and its welfare level is indicated by the lower indifference curve I_1. As welfare is measured only ordinally, it is not possible to say by how much welfare is reduced, but a measure can be established in terms of real income. By definition, the consumers are indifferent between the bundles of goods at the no-trade point A (X_1', X_2') and point E (X_1'', X_2''), also lying on indifference curve I_1. Assuming that the indifference curves are homothetic, the slopes of the relative price curves through point B $(p_2^i p_2^i)$ and through point E (p_1^i, p_1^i) are the same, as B and E lie on a ray from the origin. The distance between the two relative price or real income curves measures the reduction of real income arising from the exclusion from international trade. Measured in terms of good X_1, the relative loss is $(X_1^c - X_1'')/X_1^c$, and in terms of good X_2 it is $(X_2^c - X_2'')/X_2^c$.

Figure 6.1 allows us to identify the factors that determine the size of the real income loss from boycotts. The loss resulting from the impossibility of trading internationally will be the larger, and therefore sanctions will be more effective, when:

1 the production possibility curve F is more curved (more concave) and therefore more could be gained by engaging in international trade because of the advantages of specialization – or more is lost when such trade is prevented. On the other hand, a flat production possibility curve means that not much can be gained by specializing in the production of the good (here of X_1) with relative advantage. A strongly concave production possibility curve indicates that the country's production structure is inflexible;

2 the indifference curves I are more curved (more convex). A strong curvature of indifference curves means that the consumers are fixed on a particular combination of goods, and are unwilling to move away from this combination. (On the other

hand, when the indifference curves are flat the consumers are
quite ready to substitute one good for another.) A strong
curvature therefore indicates that the consumer preferences
are inflexible;
3 the country's imports and exports were larger before the
blockade.

Economic theory thus draws our attention to the importance of
flexibility in both production and consumption. Economic sanctions will impose a sizeable welfare and real income loss on the
population of the country boycotted only if its production and
consumption cannot be easily adjusted to the interruption in
trade.

Sanctions against Rhodesia

The trade model developed can be applied to illustrate the effect
of economic boycotts on Rhodesia, as Zimbabwe was called at
that time. The sanctions imposed first by the UK and then by
the United Nations were increased in stages after the white
Rhodesian government unilaterally declared its country's independence in November 1965. The aim was to force Rhodesia to
give up its repressive domestic policies towards the black
population. In their final form (UN Security Council Resolution
of 29 May 1968), the sanctions were intended to stop *completely*
the movement of goods and factors of production to and from
Rhodesia (see Porter 1978).
    The conditions for these sanctions to be effective seemed to be
extremely favourable. There were few countries more strongly
dependent on trade than Rhodesia: exports amounted to almost
40 per cent, and imports to 30 per cent, of GNP in 1965.
Accordingly, trade was extremely important and condition
3 above was met. Production and exports were heavily concentrated on tobacco (and a few minerals), so that the productive
structure seemed to have little flexibility, meeting condition 1.
Finally, the dominating white consumers did not seem ready to
change their consumption habits, so condition 2, of inflexible
preferences, also seemed to be fulfilled.
    Events showed, however, that the flexibility of Rhodesia's
production and consumption patterns was underrated (see

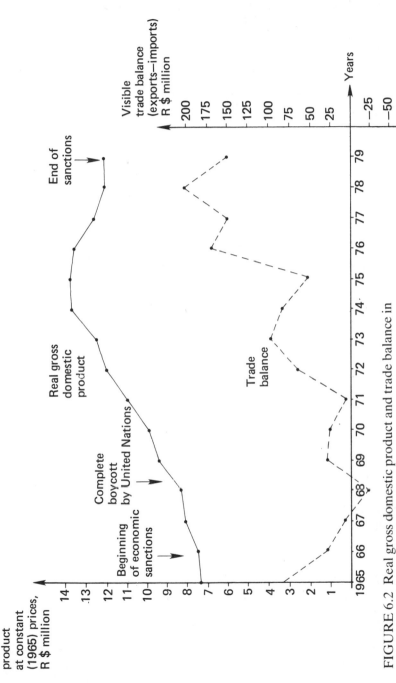

FIGURE 6.2 Real gross domestic product and trade balance in Rhodesia during economic sanctions, 1965–79.
(*Source:* Renwick, 1981, tables VI and VII; selected figures.)

Renwick 1981). In the first year after the sanctions were imposed (1966), two-thirds of Rhodesia's former export markets were officially subject to embargo. Exports fell substantially; their value declined by more than one-third, from R$320 million to R$200 million; and the trade balance worsened (but stayed positive). Gross domestic product, however, increased by almost 2 per cent in real terms over the previous year. The development of real GDP and of the trade balance is shown in figure 6.2. Employment declined, but the burden fell exclusively on the African population.

Figure 6.2 and the growth rates of real GDP shown in table 6.1 indicate that Rhodesia's economic conditions certainly did not worsen, but rather improved, in the first two years (1966–7) after the boycott began. Real GDP increased by almost 5 per cent per year, an astonishing performance. Equally surprisingly, the good growth performance was achieved with near price stability. The boycotts had an effect mainly on the sectoral composition of production. Tobacco, Rhodesia's main export product, was strongly hit at the beginning of the sanctions.

TABLE 6.1   Average annual growth rate of real gross domestic product in Rhodesia during economic sanctions: selected periods, 1966–79

Short-run impact (first two years), 1966–7	Medium-term impact (third to eighth years), 1968–74	Oil price rise and world recession 1975–9
4.9%	7.8%	−2.3%

Source: own calculations on the basis of Renwick (1981), table VI.

Not only in the short run, but also in the long run, sanctions impaired Rhodesia's aggregate economy very little. Figure 6.2 shows that real national income (GDP) steadily rose until 1974, with an average annual growth rate of as much as 7.8 per cent (table 6.1). The trade balance was negative in only one year, 1968 (mainly because of an exceptionally bad harvest), but a strong trend of increasing surpluses is indicated.

The oil price rise of the OPEC countries at the end of 1973 and the resulting widespread world economic recession affected Rhodesia's economy much more strongly than did the economic sanctions. Another factor causing a worsening of economic conditions was the burden imposed by the anti-terrorist operations, which led to an enormous increase in public expenditure. Starting in 1975, real GDP began to decline (figure 6.2), by an average annual amount of 2.3 per cent in the period 1975–9. Again, the main burden of this reduction in the standard of living had to be borne by the rural African population.

Despite the worsening economic conditions, the end of Rhodesia was due to *political* influences, especially the independence of Mozambique, which greatly helped the guerilla movement. In January 1979 a new constitution allowing for majority rule was accepted, and in the parliamentary elections of April 1979 the black leader Bishop Muzorewa was chosen prime minister. In December 1979 the sanctions were officially lifted.

TABLE 6.2   Sources of economic growth in Rhodesia before (1955–65) and after (1965–75) economic sanctions

	1955–60	1960–65	1965–70	1970–75
	%	%	%	%
Growth rate of real GDP	4.4	1.6	4.8	6.8
due to:				
– physical capital	3.1	–0.3	0.3	2.9
– white labour	1.8	0	0.9	0.9
– black labour	0.4	0	0.6	1.0
Residual	–0.9	1.9	3.0	2.0

Source: Porter (1978), table 2 (rounded figures).

It could be argued that the analysis presented is not convincing, as the influence of the economic sanctions is not isolated. In principle, it could be true that the boycotts *were* effective, since without them the Rhodesian growth performance would have been even better. To counter this argument, an attempt has been made to identify the sources of growth (Porter 1978). The results are shown in table 6.2.

In the period 1955–60, real GDP rose at an annual rate of 4.4 per cent. Of this growth, 3.1 per cent can be attributed to the growth (and productivity increase) of physical capital, and 1.8 per cent and 0.4 per cent to the increased input (and productivity) of white and black labour, respectively. The residual (unexplained by factor inputs) or exogenous productivity increase amounts to –0.9 per cent per year, which may be attributed to unidentified factors such as technical progress. This residual factor was 1.9 per cent in the following five-year time period (1960–5) before sanctions were imposed. One would expect that the economic sanctions imposed after 1966 would *reduce* this residual, because the outside interference into foreign trade is an influence depressing overall productivity. A look at table 6.2, however, shows, that this is not the case: the residual for 1965–70 is 3 per cent and for 1970–5, 2 per cent per year, which is higher than in the years before the imposition of the sanctions. This result would suggest that the boycotts resulted in a productivity increase.

The many studies undertaken on the effects of the economic sanctions against Rhodesia (see in particular Doxey 1980) almost invariably come to the conclusion that they inflicted little economic hardship beyond a brief transition period. In a detailed study (Knorr 1975, pp. 150–60) of 22 cases of economic sanctions, most of which occurred after the Second World War, it is found that they clearly failed in 13 cases; a compromise settlement was achieved in 3 cases, and the outcome is ambiguous in 2 cases. Only 4 cases can be considered successful, always owing to the exceptional circumstance that the country boycotted found it *completely* impossible to trade with other countries.

POLITICAL CONDITIONS FOR EFFECTIVE ECONOMIC SANCTIONS

The ineffectiveness of blockades in the case of Rhodesia and other countries may be due not only to the fact that the boycotted economies have a much greater flexibility of production and consumption than is usually supposed, but also to the fact that any adverse economic effect may bring about unintended reactions in the internal political situation. In so far as the economy is harmed by the sanctions, the costs fall on the population of the country boycotted, and not on its political leaders. As the hardships are brought about by aggressive outside intervention, the population tends not to turn against its own government but rather to rally to its support against the outside aggressor. As a result, there is more social and political cohesion within the country and less dissent. The government therefore is in a stronger position than before. The population and the government feel united in their sense of isolation, which serves to weaken rather than strengthen external influence. This, indeed, is what happened when the League of Nations imposed economic sanctions on Italy: the immediate effect was a strengthening of popular support for the Mussolini regime.

REASONS FOR INEFFECTIVENESS

The discussion of the organizational, economic and political conditions for effective economic sanctions suggests that they will rarely be met in reality, as they are very demanding. Nevertheless, sanctions may still have *some* effect on the intended direction, even if some or all conditions are violated. Research (e.g. Seeler 1982) indicates three main reasons why economic sanctions have not reached, or even satisfactorily approximated, their intended goals.

1 There is usually a considerable time distance between the decision to undertake sanctions and their legal and administrative implementation. This allows the boycotted country, and also those groups within the boycotting country expecting to lose from the policy, to organize counter-measures and to exploit fully the possibilities offered by flexible production and consumption patterns.

2 The main reason for the ineffectiveness lies in the fact that such far-reaching interventions into international trade as boycotts create considerable profit opportunities for boycott-breakers. This incentive exists both for countries as a whole and for individual firms. Those who find legal or illegal ways to get round the embargo, in particular the many ways of indirect trade, can reap unusually high profits.

3 Internal resistance in the boycotting country tends gradually to erode the determination of the government to apply the sanctions effectively. The main reason for this is that the costs of sanctioning tend to increase over time, while the benefits remain vague or do not exist at all.

COSTS FOR THE BOYCOTTER

Trade is beneficial for all parties: this is the classical wisdom of economic theory. The reverse equally holds: an interruption of trade hurts both the boycotted and the boycotting nation. In addition to the welfare losses arising from the reduction or stop in trade, a boycotting country is also reducing its own productive efficiency, because the increased state intervention into its economy, in the form of export and import regulations and controls, hampers economic activity. These counter-productive effects worsen the relative position of the boycotting nation.

Effects of sanctions that benefit the boycotted nation may lie in the economic or political sphere. In the case of Rhodesia, as has been noted, they resulted in an increase in overall productivity. This may be due to the fact that an exogenous shock to the economy may awaken entrepreneurial spirit and allow efficiency-increasing measures to be taken that were formerly opposed by interest groups, in particular by trade unions. Also, sanctions force the boycotted nation to diversify its production, and provide protection to infant industries. This was the case in Rhodesia, which quickly built up a manufacturing sector in response to the boycott.

The counter-productive effects in the political sphere may be even more important. Economic pressure as such does not produce the incentives necessary for a country to change its policy in the direction desired by the boycotters; for that purpose the boycotted country must be shown, and be offered, an alternative course of action from that currently pursued. This alternative must be considered by the government and population of the boycotted country as a lesser evil, or even as an advantage.

WHY ARE ECONOMIC SANCTIONS IMPOSED?

The discussion on the one hand of the conditions necessary for boycotts to have the intended political effects, and of the extent to which they can be expected to be met, and on the other hand of the costs that the boycotting country (or collectivity) has to carry, suggests that, from the standpoint of a country as a whole, a boycott is unlikely to be a profitable enterprise, at least in times of peace. The (major) goal of imposing economic hardship, and thereby inducing the country that is boycotted to undertake a more desirable policy, is rarely achieved. Why, then, is such an unsuccessful policy so often undertaken?

The unfavourable benefit–cost ratio of economic sanctions for the country imposing the boycott does not mean that it may not be advantageous for the *government* to embark on such a policy. Quite often, the population will want the government to take a strong stand on foreign policy, in particular with current and former world powers (such as the United States and the UK). The government has three broad options: to do nothing, to take some form of military action, or to apply economic penalties. In order not to lose votes to the opposition, who could accuse the government of indecision and weakness, the politicians in power have to take *some* action, thereby excluding the first option. Short of war, the threat and imposition of economic sanctions is often the only course of action left open to them. Such action also gives the government the chance to take a principled stand and to make its fundamental position clear, a behaviour that the electorate tends to honour in the international field.

The benefit–cost relationship of boycotts to a government thus differs from that which would apply to the country as a whole. The government reaps greater benefits and has to carry smaller costs, at least in the short run. This difference between the national and the governmental benefit–cost ratio applies only as long as the voters fall prey to 'symbolic politics', and are not fully informed and aware of the small effectiveness of economic sanctions.

Another interpretation not relying on failures of information would be that both the voters and government in this instance do not want to reason consequentially (i.e. to calculate the outcome of their actions), but rather value the very action of protesting by imposing the boycott. The incentive for a government to join in collective sanctions is even greater, because there are additional benefits in terms of international solidarity, while it can hope to have other nations shoulder the cost of such actions.

Economic sanctions provide an interesting example of the

interaction of economics and politics in the international sphere. Boycotts have little effect because the organization is difficult, and because the boycotted country's economy is usually flexible enough to adjust production and consumption. Even in so far as sanctions are economically effective, this is unlikely to transform into the policies intended by the boycotting country.

But there is a *paradox*. Economic sanctions will be used in the future because they are relatively the best action for a government. It can be predicted that boycotts will take place regularly, but that each boycott will be maintained only over a limited period and often will subside rather quickly. This is because the groups that have to carry the main internal burden of the economic sanctions, if well organized, will lobby for a weakening of the boycotts. The producers of export goods in particular will argue that they are losing export markets for their goods, and that they have a disadvantage relative to producers in other countries that do not participate in the boycott, or interpret it less vigorously. The benefits of the sanctions in terms of international policy being rather small (if they exist at all), the government will have to compare the political weight of the groups benefiting from the boycotts – mainly the import-competing home producers, which are isolated from competition by the boycotted country – with the political weight of the above mentioned groups (exporters), which increasingly suffer from the boycotts. The best strategy for the government is at first to maintain the boycott in order not to lose face, but to grant more and more exceptions, until finally everybody knows that the economic sanctions are completely useless and they are lifted.

This rise and gradual weakening of economic sanctions predicted by economic theory may be termed 'international political cycle', in analogy to the well-known 'political business cycle' produced within a country.

CONCLUSION

Economic sanctions are often used as a means of foreign policy both by individual countries and by collective institutions such as the United Nations. In order to function at all, they must be backed by a broad enough number of countries, which presupposes that the free-rider problem inherent in collective actions, as well as internal pressures of domestic interest groups negatively affected by the boycott, are durably overcome.

The administrative organization must apply the embargoes quickly once they are decided upon. The boycotts must not have any leaks and must be effectively controlled. The harm done by boycotts in terms of welfare and real income losses is larger, the less flexible are production and consumers' preferences, and the more strongly the country in question depends on trade. Experience and empirical research especially for the case of Rhodesia in 1966–79 show that boycotts have hardly ever been successful in the sense of imposing great economic hardship on the boycotted nation.

Most economic sanctions have proved to be ineffective because the boycotted countries can adjust their production and consumption, and also can maintain international trade indirectly – a possibility that is regularly opened up owing to the high profit opportunities created. The boycotting nation experiences considerable cost too, especially as a continuation of international trade would be beneficial to all participants. Economic sanctions also have counter-productive economic and political effects, weakening the relative position of the boycotting nation to the boycotted nation(s).

While trade wars almost always have an unfavourable benefit–cost ratio for the boycotting country as a whole, this need not be so for the government of that country, since it may profit in terms of votes from a population that wants it to take a strong stand on foreign policy. As the benefits of economic sanctions turn out to be rather small or even non-existent, while the costs for particular groups in the boycotting nations tend to increase, the government tends to loosen the sanctions over time. This creates an 'international political cycle'.

FURTHER READING

WORKS MENTIONED IN THE TEXT

Doxey, Margaret P. (1980), *Economic Sanctions and International Enforcement*, 2nd ed. London: Macmillan.

Hasse, Rolf (1977), *Wirtschaftliche Sanktionen als Mittel der Aussenpolitik*. Berlin: Duncker and Humblot.

Knorr, Klaus (1975), *The Political Economy of International Relations*. New York: Basic Books.

Medlicott, William N. (1952–9), *The Economic Blockade. History of the Second World War, UK Civil Series* (2 vols). London: HMSO and Longmans Green.

Porter, Richard C. (1978), 'Economic Sanctions: The Theory and the Evidence from Rhodesia'. *Journal of Peace Science*, 3 (Spring), 93–110.

Renwick, Robin (1981), *Economic Sanctions*. Cambridge, Mass.: Center for International Affairs, Harvard University.

Seeler, Hans-Joachim (1982), 'Wirtschaftssanktionen als zweifelhaftes Instrument der Aussenpolitik'. *Europa-Archiv*, 20, 611–18.

WORKS RELATING TO ASPECTS DISCUSSED

Two standard books on economic warfare are

Adler-Karlsson, Gunnar (1968), *Western Economic Warfare 1947–1967: A Case Study in Foreign Economic Policy*. Stockholm: Almqvist & Wicksell.

Wan, Yuan-li (1952), *Economic Warfare*. Englewood Cliffs, NJ: Prentice-Hall.

Particularly interesting treaties on economic sanctions are

Baldwin, David A. (1971), 'The Power of Positive Sanctions', *World Politics*, 24 (October), 19–38.

Galtung, Johan (1967), 'On the Effects of International Economic Sanction With Examples From the Case of Rhodesia'. *World Politics*, 19 (April), 378–416.

More modern contributions are

Losman, Donald L. (1980), *International Economic Sanctions: The Case of Cuba, Israel and Rhodesia*. Albuquerque: University of New Mexico Press.

Hufbauer, Gary Clyde and Schott, Jeffrey J., (1983), *Economic Sanctions in Support of Foreign Policy Goals*. Washington DC.: Institute for International Economics.

The possibility that a shake-up in the form of externally imposed international economical sanctions increases a country's overall productivity reminds one of the thesis that the existence of established interest groups slows down economic growth because they prevent the necessary structural changes. See

Olson, Mancur (1982), *The Rise and Decline of Nations. Economic Growth, Stagflation. and Social Rigidities*. New Haven and London: Yale University Press.

It may be argued that the main effect of economic sanctions is not when they are applied but when they are *threatened*. If the threat is credible, the threatened country must take action to guard against this anticipated risk, which will bind resources that could be used profitably elsewhere. See e.g.

Hallet, Hughes A.J. and Brandsma, Andries S. (1983), 'How Effective Could Sanctions Against the Soviet Union Be?' *Weltwirtschaftliches Archiv*, 119, 498–522.

The underlying assumption of the analysis that the leaders of countries compare the expected benefits and costs of alternative actions, i.e. act rationally, is applicable not only to economics but also to warfare, as shown by

de Mesquita, Bruce Bueno (1981), *The War Trap*. New Haven and London: Yale University Press.

Mesquita uses expected utility maximization to explain the occurrence and intensity of military confrontations.

7

Why Is International Co-operation So Difficult?

GLOBAL COMMONS ARE DESTROYED

A great many people feel deeply concerned about the mass killing of whales; they fear that it will lead to a complete annihilation of this mammal. To prevent this from happening they demand an immediate stop to whaling. Nobody should be allowed to kill whales.

The problem with such demands is that the whaling nations (today mainly Japan and the Soviet Union) are sovereign states, and are not inclined to give up this profitable activity.

The International Whaling Commission, which first met in 1949, found it impossible to reduce the killing. The Commission had no means to enforce compliance to the restrictions established. As the whale population declined further and competition for remaining whales intensified, the whalers even forced the Commission to rescind some of the protective regulations it had earlier established. The whaling nations were therefore not even capable of complying with an agreement that was undoubtedly in their own interest. It is not surprising that the concerns of the protectionists – who were not involved in the negotiations – had no effect at all.

However, the uninhibited catch led to such a rapid decline in the whale population that the nations with whaling fleets finally found it to be in their own interest to seek a convention by which to limit whaling.

In 1975, by which time some subspecies of whales had become extinct, 16 member-states of the International Whaling Commission were able to agree on a rule prohibiting the hunting of those whales that are believed to be below the level of the 'maximum sustainable yield' (i.e. the size of the whale population that allows the largest possible catch in the long run). Annual quotas are now to be set in order to maintain the sustained yield.

This agreement was neither quite voluntary nor the result of 'enlightened self-interest'. Rather, the United States (where the protectionist movement has become a political factor to reckon with) threatened to cut off its fisheries imports from the two nations that most strongly objected, the Soviet Union and Japan. The problem has not been solved even today, however, because nations outside the International Whaling Commission, such as Taiwan, Korea and China, seized the opportunity presented by IWC restricted members' catches to embark on large whaling operations of their own.

Whaling is just one example of how difficult international co-operation is in the context of 'global commons'. A 'common' is a resource with badly defined or non-existent property rights. This results in overuse and leads in the long run to a destruction of the resource. Global commons are of great importance in the international context where they apply to deep sea fishing, ocean mining, pollution of the seas and the air and (which will be of increasing importance in the future) the use of outer space and of the orbit spectrum.

INTERNATIONAL PUBLIC GOODS AND FREE-RIDING

Access to a common has been unrestricted by tradition: every individual is free to use and exploit the natural resource of a common property independently of others. In particular, the seas and oceans have been considered by international law to be *res communes, res publicae* and *res nullius* (collective and public goods of nobody's property). Free use does not create a problem as long as the resource is so widely available that the users do not interfere with each other. When the resource is scarce, however, access must be limited in some way in order to prevent congestion and overuse; but no one user has an incentive, or can afford, to take care of the overall scarcity as long as the user-price is zero.

To take whaling as an example, no country will be prepared

unilaterally to restrict its catch if it knows that the result will only be to provide other nations with better fishing opportunities, and not to protect the whale population as a whole. The same applies, for example, to the exploitation of the oil fields in the ocean if they are treated as a common property resource; each firm or nation has an incentive to maximize the rate of exploitation without taking the scarcity of oil into account, because if it does not, the other firms or nations will simply exploit it themselves.

This behaviour also leads to a waste of resources (an inefficient allocation) because of overinvestment. It has been empirically shown, for example, that 80 per cent of labour and capital engaged in salmon fishing in Alaska was redundant during the 1950s, and that the fishing fleet in the Pacific Ocean was tripled in the same period, while the yield on salmon increased by only 50 per cent (Crutchfield and Pontecorvo 1979). In both cases, too many factors of production were used to hunt the rapidly shrinking fish population, because it is a global common that induces a race for as rapid an exploitation as possible.

The problem of overuse and destruction of global common property resources is a feature of international economic interdependence that creates public goods and externalities. It therefore extends beyond natural resources and includes areas such as collective security. In all these cases the individual independent actor has little incentive to take an overall view and to provide the public good (which may be the protection of whales and fish, the preservation of oil resources, or the common interest in the security of a group of nations) but rather tends to act as a free-rider. There are various other aspects of the international economy that it may be useful to examine from the point of view of public goods, as well as the tendency for free-riding, in which a public good is available to all, irrespective of whether everyone has contributed to its supply.

Thus, law and order can be considered a public good forming an important complement to foreign trade. Its absence may lead to a serious disruption in international exchange and to consequent welfare losses. The institution of a common state composed of previously independent regional units may also be looked upon as a public good. The high costs arising when it does *not* exist may be illustrated by the example of Germany in 1870 (Kindleberger

1978): then, there were 1700 tariff boundaries with 300 rulers levying tolls as they pleased. No wonder the advantages of trade exchange could not be exploited to any reasonable degree. Trade liberalization thus may also be looked at as a public good. The same applies to the existence of a national currency as a unit of account or measure, as well as more generally to any kind of international standardization that serves to reduce transaction costs and achieve economies of scale through product interchangeability.

The public goods problem arising in international co-operation and the concomitant free-rider behaviour may be illustrated with the help of figure 7.1 (Olson 1971). Assume for simplicity that there are only two countries, A and B. The amount of the public good X provided by a co-operation between the two countries (e.g. the intensity of pollution control or the size of an international military force) is shown on the horizontal axis. The value of the supply of X from the point of view of country A is given by curve V_A, of country B by V_B. According to the figure, country A values the good more than country B. Curve V indicates the aggregate value $(V=V_A+V_B)$ of good X. The cost of providing

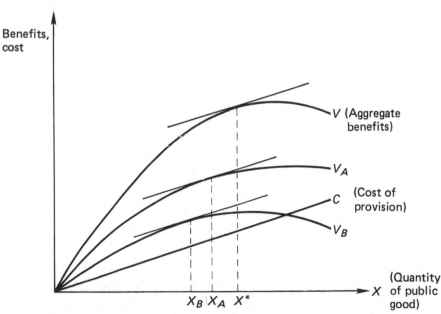

FIGURE 7.1 The problems of public good supply.

the good is given by the cost curve C. For both countries combined, it would be worthwhile to supply the quantity X^*, where total marginal value (benefit) dV/dX equals marginal cost dC/dX. If country A were acting in isolation, it would supply the quantity X_A, where $dV_A/dX = dC/dX$; and if country B acted in isolation it would supply X_B, where $dV_B/dX = dC/dX$.

But the interdependence between the two countries completely changes the picture. If country A supplied X_A, country B would supply *nothing*, because, X being a public good, country B has full access to it and does not have to incur the cost of providing it: country B acts as a (complete) free-rider. If X denotes the size of an international military force, country A would put it up alone, and country B would not find it necessary to do anything but would nevertheless be fully protected.

This situation is, however, no equilibrium. Country A resents B's free-riding for obvious reasons and will threaten to supply only a limited amount of the public good, or at least less than the quantity desired by B. This threat in turn will induce country B to propose to provide a certain amount of the public good, which in turn will motivate country A to react. The interdependence in the behaviour of the two nations thus turns the provision of the public good into a *bargaining* problem, the outcome of which is difficult and often impossible to predict.

SOLUTIONS TO INTERNATIONAL FREE-RIDING

Countries are well aware that international co-operation in providing public goods is difficult to achieve. Efforts have therefore been made to overcome or mitigate the free-rider incentive in order to continue to benefit from international public goods. Solutions have been sought in three different ways; they are not mutually exclusive, but may reinforce each other under favourable conditions.

1   Private goods can be offered selectively to the co-operating nations, making it individually worthwhile for a country to join and to participate in the financing of the international public good. Creating such selective incentives is an important prerequisite for governments agreeing to join in international acts of co-operation. Considerable effort therefore should be made by

all participants to transform, as far as possible, the international public good into *private* goods.

This is not always easy, because not all international public goods can be redefined so that exclusive benefits will accrue to individual countries. An example of where this is possible (up to a point) concerns military alliances. An individual country's contribution to the common defence effort (the public good) is partly transformed into a private good if the troops that are contributed to the alliance are used to defend the territorial integrity of the nation concerned, and if, under special circumstances, they may also be used for internal national purposes such as to combat riots. It follows that international co-operation will take place if at the same time it serves to produce national goods; collective action is used partly to further individual (national) benefits.

The association of the international public good with national private goods means that it becomes possible for the nations to bargain on a *quid pro quo* basis: a country will receive benefits only if in turn it is prepared to offer benefits to the other countries. The countries involved do not have to face the 'grand' decision of whether or not to participate in the provision of the international public good. Rather, the creation of associated private goods makes it possible to proceed sequentially in mutually beneficial steps. This quasi-'market' in terms of private goods produces the atmosphere of trust necessary for the international public good to remain linked with the private goods (see Frei 1982, with empirical tests).

A special type of private good that induces nations to participate in the provision of an international public good is the desire to influence the *nature* of the public good. A country that free-rides has no say in this respect. In the case of a military alliance, for example, it cannot influence the size, structure or geographical distribution of the military forces or appoint nationals to leading positions. This constitutes an incentive for all countries to participate, and perhaps to a generally 'acceptable' degree, but it does not reduce the incentive to contribute less than the (marginal) benefits that the international public good produces.

2 *Coercion* can be attempted. This possibility for forming and maintaining co-operation is often difficult or impossible to put into practice in the international context. The member-countries

are unwilling to give up their sovereignty. Therefore, assuming (as is sometimes done) that coercion is possible defines away the basic problem of international co-operation. For instance, it does not help much to call for a world government that would force the super-powers to disarm, since the super-powers are not willing to yield any of their power to another institution.

3 *Rules* or *constitutional agreements* laying down the conditions for co-operation can be sought. Such agreements set down the 'rules of the game' that the participating nations are willing to accept in the state of uncertainty about the future. An example is an agreement about the rules for dealing with plane hijackers, for instance to send them back to the country they started from. This form of international co-operation may well benefit all countries, as they do not know the particular instances of hi-jacking that will arise in the future. As the countries have to decide behind the 'veil of ignorance', they agree to the general rule because it allows for the provision of the international public good of air security that is advantageous to each one of them.

The rule established must lead to a Pareto-superior move according to the expectations of all the actors. Only under these conditions will voluntary co-operation come about among the countries involved. Suitable conditions are not easy to find. Once a rule or constitution has been agreed upon, the problem consists in making sure the rules are observed and in overcoming the incentives of the individual nations to corrupt the agreement. In the above example of plane hijacking rules, a country that finds it advantageous to support the agreement *ex ante* may want to break the rule in a particular case, for instance when the hijacker absconds from another country for political reasons and applies for asylum. The countries interested in this particular form of air security must be ready to bind themselves in the initial state of uncertainty in order not to admit such exceptions, which would destroy the co-operation and the international public good of air security.

In general, it is easier to find and to maintain co-operation agreements among a *small group* of nations. Free-riding is not as easy here as in large groups, because the nations find it easier to monitor each other's behaviour. A country breaking a rule is more easily found out and punished in some way or another, sometimes by simply ostracizing such damaging behaviour. 'Norms of reciprocity' do exist between nations that interact with each other. Indeed, it has been shown empirically that small, especially regional, international organizations are more successful than large ones: the performance of 20 multilateral international organizations correlates negatively with the number of states being members (Russet and Sullivan 1971).

AREAS OF INTERNATIONAL CO-OPERATION

Three important areas will be discussed in which co-operation over the provision of international public goods is sought and where free-riding exists, and where rules or 'constitutions' have been used in an attempt to overcome the difficulties. They are international (military) alliances, the international monetary system, and global common property resources.

INTERNATIONAL ALLIANCES

Owing to its more extensive territory, a large country requires a larger amount of military expenditures than a small country in order to achieve the same level of protection. Similarly, a rich country runs a greater risk of being attacked than a poor country, and will therefore benefit more from defence. The benefit curve for military expenditures of a large and rich country will everywhere lie above that of a small and poor country. In terms of figure 7.1, country A can be interpreted as being a large and rich country, country B a small and poor country, and X the public good 'security' achieved by military expenditures. If the large, rich country has committed itself to making large outlays for this public good, the small, poor nation (or nations) will have an incentive to spend less on this good than they would in the absence of the large country. In military alliances the small and poor countries spend a smaller *share* of their GNP for the provision of the alliance's collective security than do the large and rich countries.

This proposition may be empirically tested for NATO countries (see Olson and Zeckhauser 1966) and for the Warsaw Pact members. According to the theory advanced, the dominating (large and rich) countries – the United States in NATO and the Soviet Union in the Warsaw Pact – are expected to make a larger defence effort, while the other members of the two military alliances have a tendency to behave as free-riders and spend less on defence. Table 7.1 lists the member-countries' defence outlays as a share of their gross domestic product.

Comparing the nations' defence efforts by their share of defence outlays in gross domestic product is questionable, however, because the definition of defence expenditure differs between nations, and not all inputs (for instance, conscription) are correctly taken into account. The figures also exclude a country's expenditure on 'civilian' goods and services that contribute indirectly to a country's defence, such as outlays for health and sports, or for diplomatic activities. Moreover, defence expenditure ratios measure the inputs and not the output of the defence effort. Differences in the *efficiency* of the military effort are therefore completely disregarded. Nevertheless, the figures are able to illustrate the predictions made by the economic theory of alliances: in both defence treaties, the dominating country spends a much higher share of GDP on defence than the other member countries. In the case of NATO the United States spent 5.9 per cent of its GDP on defence in 1981, while the other countries (with the exception of Greece) spent considerably less, the unweighted average being 3.5 per cent of GDP. In the case of the Warsaw Pact, the Soviet Union spent 8.8 per cent of GDP for military purposes, while the other member countries spent much less, the unweighted average being 2.9 per cent of GDP. The dominating country thus spent 69 per cent more than an 'average' member country in NATO, and 203 per cent more in the Warsaw Pact. In earlier years this tendency towards free-riding was equally strong: in 1973 the dominating country spent 82 per cent more in NATO and 272 per cent more in the Warsaw Pact in terms of the share of military expenditures in GDP.

Such calculations are capable of providing only a rough and approximate indication of whether the free-riding effect produced by the public good defence obtains in reality. There are a great many other factors influencing military expenditures, in the case of both the dominating and the other members of a defence

TABLE 7.1   Military expenditures as a share of gross domestic product of the member-countries of NATO and the Warsaw pact, 1980/81

	%	%
NATO (1981)		
Dominating country:		
United States		5.9
Other countries:		
Belgium	3.5	
Canada	1.8	
Denmark	2.5	
France	4.2	
FR Germany	3.4	
Greece	7.0	
Italy	2.5	
Luxembourg	1.1	
Netherlands	3.2	
Norway	2.9	
Portugal	3.6	
Turkey	4.9	
United Kingdom	5.0	
Unweighted average		3.5
Warsaw Pact (1980)		
Dominating country:		
Soviet Union		8.8
Other countries:		
Bulgaria	3.2	
Czechoslovakia	3.1	
German D.R.	4.3	
Hungary	2.3	
Poland	2.9	
Romania	1.7	
Unweighted average		2.9

Source: Calculated on the basis of Stockholm International Peace Research Institute SIPRI, Taylor & Francis Ltd, London/New York, 1983, table 7.A.4, p. 170.

alliance. Military expenditures are an international public good to a limited extent only: they clearly also serve purely *national* purposes. This is apparent from the shares of military expenditures of the individual countries, which exhibit a considerable variance – in NATO they range from the 7 per cent of Greece to the 1.1 per cent of Luxembourg or the 1.8 per cent of Canada; in the Warsaw Pact form the 4.3 per cent of the German Democratic Republic to the 1.7 per cent of Romania.

While such country-specific effects should be controlled for, the figures and calculations presented in table 7.1 suggest that they are not so strong as to completely overshadow the free-riding effect hypothesized. It may be concluded that the results support the notion that the 'average' members of defence alliances such as NATO or the Warsaw Pact make a disproportionally small defence effort, while the dominating large countries (the United States and the Soviet Union, respectively) bear a disproportionally large burden.

Free-riding behaviour can also be observed in the United Nations: the richest members, who presumably have the greatest interest in the maintenance of peace by a collective international organization, are by far the greatest contributors. The United States pays a third of the UN budget, and when the organization was founded had to fight hard to avoid having to pay one-half or more. The five permanent members of the Security Council (USA, USSR, UK, France and China) pay two-thirds of the budget, and 20 per cent of the members contribute 90 per cent (Kennedy 1979).

INTERNATIONAL MONETARY SYSTEMS

All nations engaged in international trade and finance depend on the existence of a monetary order that enables them to make the necessary payments. A monetary order consists of a set of rules that are to be kept by all countries, such as the former gold standard or (after the Second World War) the Bretton Woods system.

These rules, if well designed, are advantageous to all, but the incentives to deviate from them are also marked. It is therefore necessary not only to devise an international monetary scheme that is potentially beneficial to all nations, but also to consider explicitly the benefits and costs to the *individual* participating nations. This aspect has been overlooked by the many proposals made for international monetary reform, which usually (implicitly) assume that there is an 'international benevolent dictator' who will put them into effect.

A common monetary system, or *monetary integration*, yields various benefits to the countries participating. The most important are a reduction of the uncertainty produced by fluctuations in exchange rates among the national currencies of members of the monetary union, as well as the cost savings of mutual conversions of currencies within the union for the purpose of trade and travel. These benefits are closely linked to the functions of money as unit of account, a medium of exchange and a store of value. They are international public goods in the sense that all the members of the monetary union benefit from the common money. The benefits of a monetary union can, however, be withheld to a large extent from non-members. There is no rivalry with respect to a 'consumption' of the benefits (i.e., if one member benefits this does not reduce the benefits going to other members), but there *is* exclusiveness.

These special conditions have been studied in the context of the *economic theory of clubs* (Buchanan 1965). In contrast to the benefits, the cost of monetary integration has to be carried nationally. The most important disadvantage of joining a monetary union is that the level of unemployment and the rate of inflation can no longer be determined nationally. The national governments dislike such loss of control or of sovereignty, because it reduces their chances to influence the economy according to their own purposes, in particular to secure their re-election. These costs are concrete, while the benefits appear as vague and abstract. Moreover, the costs of the sacrifice of domestic economic objectives and of an independent monetary policy come quickly, while it takes time for the benefits to materialize. Owing to the publicness, delayed appearance and vagueness of benefits, and the private, national nature and clear visibility of the cost, few successful monetary integrations are to be expected to be formed and maintained purely for *economic* motives.

The history of the national unification movements suggests, indeed, that monetary integrations are formed and successfully maintained only if they are preceded, and accompanied, by a strong political movement, as well as by customs unions where the benefit–cost relationship is more favourable from the point of view of individual countries in the early period of unification. The German Zollverein, led by Prussia after 1871, removed the customs barriers between the member-states, but numerous currencies were still issued by local authorities. In 1875 the Prussian Bank was reorganized as the Reichsbank, but it was only one of 33 banks of issue. Only in 1935 was the sole right of issue given to the Reichsbank.

In Italy, the political unification under the leadership of the Kingdom of Sardinia (1861) led to a customs union whereby the tariffs of Sardinia were extended over the whole nation. There was no monetary unification, however: many different monies coexisted at the same time. The various banks were unwilling to give up their seignorage rights. *De facto* monetary integration came about only in 1893, when the Sardinian National Bank became the Bank of Italy. The Bank of Italy became the central bank *de jure* even much later, in 1926 (see Hamada 1977).

These historical examples of Germany and Italy support the prediction derived from economic theory that, owing to the public good character of the benefits of monetary systems and in particular unions, they are difficult to form and maintain when it is only narrowly economic benefits and costs that matter. They also demonstrate the importance of a *political entrepreneur* – in the case of Germany, Prussia; in the case of Italy, Sardinia – who is able to reduce the power of the formerly independent political units. Once this is achieved, a combination of coercion and political incentives may be able to bring about a viable monetary system or union.

A more recent example of the importance of a political leader and a small number of participants in overcoming the public goods aspect of the benefits is the Bretton Woods system with its gold exchange standard. This was in danger of collapsing for a long time, as countries with large holdings of American dollars had an incentive to convert them into gold (as France actually did). If this conversion had been carried out worldwide, the system would have been thrown into a major crisis of confidence, doing great harm to the functioning of the international monetary system.

The gold exchange standard remained viable under the domination of the United States until the period of massive US balance of payments deficits in the 1970s. Until then there was only a small number of dollar holders who had an interest, and were able to reach an implicit agreement, in collectively assuring the stability of the system and thereby preventing a crisis. Had the dollar holdings been distributed more equally among the more than 100 countries, it is unlikely that the voluntary reluctance to convert dollars into gold would have been achieved (Willett 1977).

A similar situation exists in the international lending crises that has occurred since 1981. Under the leadership of the United States, the few industrial countries and the few very large commercial banks involved as lenders have so far managed to find agreements not only to refrain from calling back the loans from the debtor countries (such as Poland, Mexico and Brazil) unable to pay the interests and to amortize their debt, but to extend new loans so as to prevent these countries from declaring themselves bankrupt. Here again, international co-operation for the provision of a global public good was achieved because of the leadership of one country and the small-group setting referred to above.

Not all rules existing in the international monetary order have proved to be of equal importance. It is interesting to enquire why certain rules have not influenced behaviour as much as one would have expected. In the Bretton Woods system, for example, exchange rate changes were used very little, and then usually too late (Willett 1979). This is because there are forces against both devaluation and revaluation. *Devaluation* is believed to be interpreted by the voters as admitting financial failure, with negative consequences for the government in power. This is not the case, however, if the blame can be put on the previous government. Devaluations therefore tend to be made soon after a new government takes over following a general election. A particularly blatant example occurred recently in Sweden: when the Social Democrats stepped into government after their election in October 1982, they devalued the crown not less than 16 per cent on the very first day of coming into office. A *revaluation*, on the other hand, benefits the voters (consumers) through lower prices for imported goods, but greatly harms the well organized group of exporters and import-competitors, so that the government may again run into trouble.

In view of this resistance to adjust exchange rates, a government may find it advantageous to bind itself by joining an international agreement establishing freely fluctuating exchange rates. The interest groups then know that the decision about devaluation and revaluation is taken out of the hands of the government (and central bank), which removes some of the political pressure imposed on it. The government's decision to reduce its discretionary room by voluntarily binding itself may increase its power, as it is easier to refuse the demands of pressure groups to manipulate the exchange rates in favour of particular interests.

AGREEMENTS ON GLOBAL COMMON PROPERTY RESOURCES

As pointed out at the beginning of the chapter, the fundamental cause for the excessive rate of exploitation of such natural resources as fish and oil in the oceans is the difficulty of defining and policing property rights. There are three ways in which the over-use and destruction of common property resources can be prevented.

1   The first procedure is to assign newly created *property rights*. Individual nations are given the right to allocate the access to well defined parts of the resource in the way they think fit. An effective allocation method under competitive conditions is to sell the permits for exploiting the resource on an open market. The sales price of the license is a user fee which reflects the scarcity value of the natural resource. This ensures that those firms exploit the resource that are most efficient at doing so. This procedure is used in the United States to allocate the right to drill on the continental shelf and to log public forests (Wijkman 1982a).

To sell permits for exploiting natural resources on an open market has another advantage. Protectionists can directly influence the rate of exploitation by buying such permits and not using them. This means that the price and user fee for the remaining permits is, *ceteris paribus*, higher, and that less of the natural resource is used up. Such intervention could, for example, be used in the case of seals; if the country owning and effectively policing the property rights over this animal (especially Canada) set a particular quota for killing on the basis of economic and ecological considerations, environmentalists might achieve their demand for a more extensive protection of the species by themselves buying such permits, and therewith saving the lives of the corresponding number of seals.

The Third United Nations Conference on the Law of the Sea (called UNCLOS III) has agreed on the principle of 'exclusive economic zones', which grant each coastal state the exclusive management and fishing rights within 200 nautical miles from its coast. It has been estimated that 99 per cent of the total oceanic fish catch is within this zone. UNCLOS III thus proposes that the 80 coastal states have the property rights on the ocean's fishing grounds. Such a 'national enclosure' does not however, necessarily allocate property rights to the *fishing stock*, because many kinds of fish migrate from one such 'exclusive economic zone' to another; so no nation has an incentive to protect the stock. Even apart from this problem, the extended fishing limits serve to protect the domestic fishermen, and to prevent fishing by foreigners. Also, the governments often are not eager to control the total catch effectively, since such action would meet the resistance of the domestic fishing interests.

The property right over a natural resource need not be assigned to a particular nation but may implicitly be given to an international body. This is the case if liability for damage to the natural resource is imposed and monitored by an international agency. If the libability charges correctly reflect the social value of the damage, this procedure also ensures an efficient allocation of resources. This method has been suggested for preventing the pollution of the oceans by tankers (Tollison and Willett 1976). However, it requires considerable information, and it is again doubtful whether the monitoring agency has sufficient incentives to undertake its tasks effectively.

2 The second approach to preventing the destruction of

common property resources is through *regulation*. An international organization could establish the 'optimal' rate of use and
determine to what extent each nation and/or firm might participate in the exploitation. The above-mentioned, UN Conference
on the Law of the Sea proposes this procedure for the seabed and
the continental margin, which should not be any nation's
property but should be regulated 'as part of the common heritage'
and 'in the interest of mankind' by an International Seabed
Authority. This authority would limit the volume of mineral
production and assign exclusive mining rights according to
administrative principles. Seabed mining may become of great
importance in the future because of the manganese nodules on
the seabed contain such minerals as manganese, nickel, cobalt
and copper. The continental margin is expected to contain large
deposits of offshore oil and gas (Wijkman 1982b).

The orbit spectrum is another global common property
resource the use of which is now proposed to be regulated by
international organizations. The orbit spectrum resource consists
of the electromagnetic spectrum through which radio waves are
transmitted, and the orbits in space in which satellites are placed
(Wihlborg and Wijkman 1981). For a long time these resources
were not scarce, and no common property problem arose. Lately,
however, the electromagnetic spectrum as well as the orbit for
placing satellites have become increasingly congested. A UN
agency, the International Telecommunications Union, awards
frequencies on the principle of first come – first served, and free
of charge. No such organization yet exists for the allocation of
orbit space, but national governments have begun to claim
sovereignty over the outer space lying above their territories.

The main problem with the regulatory approach is that the
international organizations have little or no coercive powers, and
therefore find it difficult effectively to constrain the over-
exploitation of this particular part of the global common.

3   A third approach to the problem of the destruction of international natural resources is one of *non-interference*, and the
hope that the nations and firms in question will themselves be
able to prevent overuse by suitable co-operation. This is often a
vain hope. But the strategy of inaction recognizes that the
existence of a market failure (here, the international public goods

problem) does not necessarily constitute a case for supranational action (see Tollison and Willett 1976). International agencies are faced with a great many administrative and political problems, such as the frequent intervention of governments in the national interest. Supranational action is thus subject to 'governmental' and 'administrative' failures. As a consequence, active interference by an international organization may be worse than market failure. More often, a solution may be sought that does not require the establishment of an international organization, but is based on direct bargaining between the nations concerned.

CONCLUSION

Global common property resources are overused and destroyed if everyone has free access. A nation has little incentive to supply the international public good involved but rather acts as a free-rider. International co-operation among the countries will arise if the benefits of the international public good are transformed into private goods (selective incentives), if coercion is possible (which is rarely the case in the international area), or if the nations involved can agree on a set of rules to be observed voluntarily. To find such rules agreeable to all countries concerned is difficult, and there are many areas of international concern in which no satisfactory rules have been found. Owing to the lower costs of negotiations and reduced incentives for free-riding, it is easier to agree on rules when the number of nations involved is small.

The cost of an alliance is shared in a predictable way between the member-nations; small countries, which may benefit from the supply of international public goods (such as collective defence) provided by the activity of the large nations, tend to pay a disproportionally small share of the cost of international organizations.

There are several important areas in which international rules exist or are actively sought. The international monetary system is such a set of rules beneficial for all countries. It owes its existence partly to the fact that a small number of nations have a particularly large stake in it and are therefore willing to carry a disproportionally large share of the cost of maintaining the rules.

Global common property resources can be maintained by assigning newly created property rights to nations or to international organizations, enforcing liability for damage to the natural resources. Another possibility is to create an international agency to regulate the access to the global common property.

FURTHER READING

WORKS MENTIONED IN THE TEXT

Buchanan, James M. (1965), 'An Economic Theory of Clubs'. *Economica*, 32 (February), 1–14.

Crutchfield, James A. and Pontecorvo, Giulio (1979), *The Pacific Salmon Fisheries: A Study of Irrational Conservation*. Baltimore: Johns Hopkins University Press.

Frei, Daniel (1982), *Internationale Zusammenarbeit. Theoretische Ansätze und empirische Beiträge*. Königstein: Hain.

Hamada, Koichi (1977), 'On the Political Economy of Monetary Integration: A Public Economics Approach'. In Robert Z. Aliber (ed.), *The Political Economy of Monetary Reform*. London: Macmillan, 13–31.

Kennedy, Gavin (1979), *Burden Sharing in Nato*. London: Duckworth.

Kindleberger, Charles P. (1978), 'Government and International Trade'. *Princeton Essays in International Finance*, 129 (July).

Olson, Mancur (1971), 'Increasing the Incentives for International Co-operation'. *International Organization*, 25 (Autumn) 866–74.

Olson, Mancur and Zeckhauser, Richard (1966), 'An Economic Theory of Alliances'. *Review of Economics and Statistics*, 48, 266–79.

Russett, Bruce M. and Sullivan, Jonathan D. (1971), 'Collective Goods and International Organization'. *International Organization* 25, (Autumn), 845–65.

Tollison, Robert D. and Willett, Thomas D. (1976), 'Institutional Mechanisms for Dealing with International Externalities: A Public Choice Perspective'. In Ryan C. Amacher and Richard J. Sweeny (eds), *The Law of the Sea: US Interests and Alternatives*. Washington DC: American Enterprise Institute, 123–46.

Wihlborg, Clas G. and Wijkman, Per Magnus (1981), 'Outer Space Resources in Efficient and Equitable Use: New Frontiers for Old Principles'. *Journal of Law and Economics*, 24 (April), 23–43.

Wijkman, Per Magnus (1982a), 'Managing the Global Commons'. *International Organization*, 36 (Summer), 511–36.

Wijkman, Per Magnus (1982b), 'UNCLOS and the Redistribution of Ocean Wealth'. *Journal of World Trade Law*, 16 (January–February), 27–48.

Willett, Thomas D. (1977), *Floating Exchange Rates and International Monetary Reform*. Washington: American Enterprise Institute.

Willett, Thomas D. (1979), 'Some Aspects of the Public Choice Approach to International Economic Relations'. Paper prepared for the European University Institute Conference on 'New Economic Approaches to the Study of International Integration: Applications to Political Decision-making', Florence, May–June, 1979; Mimeo.

WORKS RELATING TO OTHER ASPECTS DISCUSSED

Various aspects of international public goods are treated in the collections of articles by

Loehr, Werner, and Sandler, Todd (eds) (1978), *Public Goods and Public Policy*. Beverly Hills: Sage.

Sandler, Todd, (ed.) (1980), *The Theory and Structures of International Political Economy*. Boulder, Colorado: Westview Press.

The role of standards in the international economy has recently been discussed by

Kindleberger, Charles P. (1983), 'Standards as Public, Collective and Private Goods'. *Kyklos*, 36, 377–96.

The constitutional approach to economic policy making is used in

Buchanan, James M. (1977), *Freedom in Constitutional Contract. Perspectives of a Political Economist*. College Station, Texas, and London: Texas A & M University Press.

Frey, Bruno S. (1983), *Democratic Economic Policy. A Theoretical Introduction*. Oxford: Martin Robertson.

The advantage of an actor in the international system to bind himself under some circumstances has been pointed out by

Schelling, Thomas (1963), *The Strategy of Conflict*. New York: Galaxy.

This book deals in a fascinating way with a great many other aspects of international political economics.

A politico-economic analysis of the international monetary system is provided, for example, by

Cohen, Benjamin J. (1977), *Organizing the World's Money: The Political Economy of International Monetary Relations*. London: Macmillan.

Problems of international common property resources are treated, for example, in

Young, Oran R. (1982), *Resource Regimes*. Berkeley: University of California Press.

8

How Do International Organizations Function?

In the last few days of December 1983 the United States publicly announced that it would leave UNESCO, one of the major sub-organizations of the United Nations. The reasons given were that this international organization tended to 'politicize' all the issues, but also that it had become a huge and inefficient bureaucracy. While the other Western industrialized nations decided to stay within the UNESCO, they made clear that they fully agreed to the charge of 'politization', 'bureaucratization' and inefficiency.

INTERNATIONAL BUREAUCRACIES

International organizations are often considered to be large bureaucracies with little, if any, useful output. Employees of such bodies are assumed mainly to shuffle around papers and memoranda, which are debated in long sessions but thereafter disappear without any noticeable effect into some drawer. This image seems to be so prevalent in the European Community, for instance, that the rather derogatory term of 'Eurocrat' is now in common use. Another complaint often heard is that much time is wasted in haggling about country shares among employees. Nationality, rather than performance, is considered to be decisive for progress in an international bureaucrat's career.

International organizations can be studied from two points of view. The first is the internal functioning of the organization, i.e.

the specific way in which the members of the organization have dealings with each other and reach decisions, and the extent to which they perform the tasks assigned to them. The second is the external behaviour of international organizations, i.e. the study of their interaction with individual nations, with each other, and with other international decision-makers (such as multinational corporations).

The internal workings of an international organization are determined strongly by the decision-making mechanisms in force, in particular by the formal voting rules that apply in the various areas. The kind of voting rules in force also has an impact on the external behaviour of an international organization.

TYPES OF VOTING RULES

It is interesting to note that many more types of voting rules are used in international organizations than in national decision-making bodies, where the simple majority rule prevails. This is because the nations participating in international bodies are reluctant to give up their sovereignty even in limited areas, and therefore are willing to join, and to co-operate actively in, an international organization only if the voting rules give it a good chance, or even a guarantee, that no (important) decision will be taken that violates its interests. The most extreme rule for guaranteeing national sovereignty is unanimity, but there are also various forms of qualified majority that serve the same purpose. Besides those time-honoured ways for reaching formal decisions, new voting rules have been devised, which are not used at present but could serve a useful function if they were applied under suitable conditions.

The problems and possibilities of using these voting rules in international organizations will now be discussed.

UNANIMITY

When all nations (or national representatives) have to agree on a decision of an international organization, the outcome will be Pareto-optimal in the sense that every nation involved will believe that the decision is to its advantage. The disadvantages of this voting rule is that it makes it difficult, time-consuming and often impossible thereby to reach an agreement, as every nation has a veto power. This situation is well known from the Security Council of the United Nations, where the five permanent members (USA, USSR, UK, France and China) may veto any decision.

The veto power may also be used for 'strategic' purposes in order to gain as much as possible from those members who are known to favour a decision. This case is endemic in the European Community (EC). The Treaty of Rome of 1957, which can be considered the constitution of the Community, specifies the decision rules to be applied for different areas. Article 158, for example, states that the members of the Commission must be appointed by unanimous vote. In general, however, article 148 determines that, apart from very special issues, the (qualified) majority rule is to be applied. In actual fact, the EC Council of Ministers (where the important decisions are taken) nevertheless have taken all major decisions by unanimous agreement. The results are as expected: the Council often requires 'marathon sessions' going on all night before reaching a compromise that can be agreed to by all. For this purpose, 'package deals' must be worked out by hundreds or thousands of national and EC officials combining several (sometimes rather unrelated) issues; in other words, log-rolling is extensively used.

Once such a deal is approved, it is extremely difficult to change, because the fine network of sub-agreements could be destroyed (Faber and Breyer 1980). Another shortcoming of the unanimity rule is that benefits of a given programme must be distributed over all member-countries, even if this is incompatible with a programme's goals. The EC regional policy is a case in point. The financial means are spread almost equally over the whole area of the Community, though they are designed for the support of lagging regions only (Cairncross et al. 1974).

It may be concluded that the unanimity rule is capable of securing the continuous support of the countries involved, but that it has to be payed for by clumsy and sometimes ill-suited decisions for the purpose at hand.

MAJORITY

If international organizations took decisions by the principle of 'one nation–one vote' the more powerful countries would not be prepared to join, or would disregard the decisions taken if they happened to be in the minority. For that reason all kinds of weighted and qualified majority rules are used. The member-countries have different amounts of votes, and/or the majority has to be greater than one-half, say three-quarters. That rule applied, for instance, in the European Community of nine countries, where France, Germany, Italy and the UK have 10 votes each, Belgium and the Netherlands 5 each, Denmark and Ireland 3 each and Luxembourg 2. Here a proposal is accepted if it gets 41 out of 58 votes (70.7 per cent). Moreover, six out of the nine countries must agree.

Weighted voting is a suitable decision mechanism when the stakes of the nations involved differ markedly. That is the case, for instance, when an international organization is founded for the provision of a global common good such as the preservation of whales. Some nations are more deeply involved than others, perhaps because part of their population depends on the income from the catch and processing of whales. The application of force being difficult or impossible, the interests of countries with higher stakes may be acknowledged by attributing more votes to them than to other countries.

The voting rights of a country or group may also be in proportion to the financial contribution made to an organization. Such a rule exists, for example, for countries represented on the Board of Governors of the International Monetary Fund. Large contributors have a greater say than small contributors; they also have a stronger interest that the international organization functions well, because they carry the largest part of the cost of the operations. While they will attempt to use the greater voting weight attributed to them to reach decisions in their own favour, they also have an incentive to ensure that the international public goods supplied by the organization are produced as efficiently as possible. In contrast, a nation contributing little to the finance of an international organization may disregard the cost side (because the others pay so much more), but nevertheless will try to benefit as much as possible.

NEW VOTING RULES

In public choice, several new ways of reaching collective decisions have been developed. Two are potentially relevant for international organizations: voting by veto and the preference-revealing mechanism.

The voting by veto rule (Mueller 1978) allows each nation to suggest its own proposition in a set of alternatives. Then each nation deletes the alternative that it dislikes most from the remaining set. The order in which the nations 'vote' is determined randomly. The final remaining alternative that has not been deleted is considered the collective choice of the international organization. Obviously, each nation has an incentive not to introduce an alternative that is strongly disliked by one or more other nations; there is even an incentive to actively consider the interests of the other nations.

This voting rule has several good features. It allows the expression of preference intensities; it brings about Pareto-optimal results (nobody can be exploited because of the veto right); and there is an unbiased revelation of preferences (i.e., there is no incentive for strategic voting). On the other hand, voting by veto is rather clumsy to administer and is open to undue influence by coalitions among subsets of nations.

In the preference-revealing mechanism (see Tideman and Tullock 1976, and Frey 1983), each nation casting a vote in a non-secret ballot may negatively affect the utility of any other nation if the collective decision would have been different had the particular nation cast its vote in favour of a different proposal. According to this voting rule, it must then pay a tax equal to the disutility imposed on other nations. This voting procedure has various advantages over a simple majority rule: it allows the expression of preference intensity; it is (nearly) Pareto-efficient; it is not subject to the voting paradox; and it provides an incentive for the participants to reveal their true preferences. The disadvantages are similar to those of voting by veto: it is subject to coalition influence; it is complicated to administer; and it is rather difficult to understand (at least for non-economists).

These newly devised voting rules may be useful in those cases in which nations are unwilling to be subjected to the traditional simple majority rule, or where traditional methods have not worked well. They obviously will not be introduced in international bodies where traditional methods of formal decision-making *are* functioning reasonably well, but they may play a useful role in breaking deadlocks under other circumstances.

The distribution of power

In chapter 5, the game-theoretic notion of a decisive or 'pivotal' member of a coalition was introduced in order to explain the distribution of foreign aid. It was argued that a nation that is capable of transforming a losing into a winning coalition can be regarded as having 'power'. The Banzhaf index (see Brams 1976) is a quantitative measure of this definition of power. It makes it possible to calculate the share of power that each nation holds according to the formal voting rule. As it measures only the power inherent in a particular distribution of votes and a particular voting rule, it is assumed that each nation acts alone, and that its preferences about the (at present unknown) future issues to be decided upon are not known. The Banzhaf index has been applied to the *ex ante* voting power of the nations in the Council of Ministers of the European Community of nine countries (Faber and Breyer 1980). The results of the calculations are shown in table 8.1.

As indicated above, the four large countries have 10 votes each, the two middle-sized countries 5, the two small countries 3 and tiny Luxembourg 2 votes, totalling 58. The table shows how the power share alters as a result of the changes in the decision rule. It may be seen that the share of votes (col. 3) deviates increasingly from the power indices as the voting rule approaches unanimity (cols 4–7). Such a table allows, for instance, the evaluation of the *ex ante* power weight of the four large EC countries as against the smaller ones. It turns out that the 69 per cent share in votes practically equals the power index when the

TABLE 8.1 Votes and power index (Banzhaf) in the council of ministers of the European community

Country (1)	Votes		Required majority			
	Absolute number (2)	Share (percentage) (3)	Simple majority (30 votes) (4)	41 votes (5)	41 votes and 6 countries (6)	Unanimity (58 votes) (7)
Germany	10 each	17.2% each	17.4% each	16.7% each	16.4% each	11.1% each
France						
United Kingdom						
Italy						
Power share, 'large' countries	(40 votes)	69%	69.5%	67%	65.5%	44.5%
Belgium	5 each	8.6% each	8.7% each	9.1% each	9.6% each	11.1% each
Netherlands						
Denmark	3 each	5.2% each	4.3% each	6.6% each	6.8% each	
Ireland						
Luxemburg	2	3.4%		1.6%	1.4%	
Power share, 'small' countries	(18 votes)	31%	30.5%	33%	34.5%	55.5%

Source: Faber and Breyer (1980), and own calculations.

voting rule is simple majority; that it falls somewhat (to 67 and 65½ per cent) when the majority becomes more qualified. In the case of the unanimity rule, every country has the same power, and the four large countries combine only 44½ per cent of the total as against 55½ per cent of the 'small' countries.

The change in voting rules at the International Monetary Fund, which became effective in 1978, has resulted in a surprising, counterintuitive change in the power structure according to the Banzhaf power index. Four major countries (Federal Republic of Germany, Japan, the Netherlands and Belgium), whose votes were increased to keep pace with their increased weight in the world economy, suffered a decline in power, while 38 countries whose votes were reduced experienced an increase in power (Dreyer and Schotter 1980).

The power index presented should be interpreted with great care. It measures only the possible influence derived from transforming a losing into a winning coalition, given a particular distribution of votes and a particular voting rule. It does not consider any other factor that may contribute to a country's power. The index is suitable for an evaluation of power only when it is completely unknown which countries will side with each other. Each logically possible coalition formation is therefore treated as being equally likely. If there is knowledge about the probable or actual voting behaviour of countries, the power distribution may look quite different. If, for instance, the four large countries in the EC form a stable coalition among themselves (see table 8.1) they are able to wield 100 per cent of the power when 30 votes are required, but must depend on other countries if 41 votes and at least six countries are required to support a proposition.

BEHAVIOURAL ASPECTS

So far, the discussion of international organizations has been concentrated on formal aspects, the formal decision-making or voting rule, and its consequences for the distribution of power. Now, the behavioural aspects will be considered.

It turns out that the typical characteristics of bureaucracies are likely to be more pronounced in international than in national settings. The main reason for this is that they have greater room for discretionary action in the former, as there is little possibility and incentive to control them. Control is difficult because the 'output' of many international organizations is badly defined and cannot usually be measured. There is little motivation to control because nobody gains by tightly monitoring an international organization; national governments would only run into trouble with other national governments if they tried to interfere with the internal workings of such institutions. Therefore they prefer to let things go and intervene only if they feel that their own nationals employed in the organization are being unfairly treated or that their national interests are being threatened by the organization's activity.

This lack of incentives to control the efficiency of international organizations is another example of the free-riding problem: organizational efficiency is an international public good, while most of the inputs are national (private) goods which have to be released from national appropriation.

Owing to the lack of effective control in an international organization, none of the levels in the hierarchy has any real incentive to work towards the 'official product' because the utility of each level depends hardly at all on its contribution. The national quotas for a great number of positions, which are a feature of many international organizations, drive a further wedge between the individual's utility and the organization's official function. This particular incentive structure leads to a growth of the international bureaucracy quite independent of the tasks to be performed, because all bureaucrats benefit from larger budgets and from a greater number of employees (see figure 8.1). International bureaucracies are also characterized by a low degree of efficiency and a profusion of red tape as the formalized internal workings of the organization become dominant. A considerable share of the budget will be used for internal purposes, and to provide side-benefits for the bureaucrats themselves.

Evidence concerning the number of staff employed by international organizations tend to support these considerations. The collection of such data meets, however, with considerable

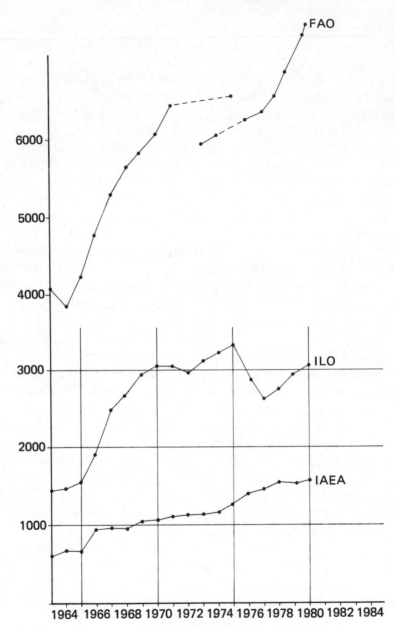

FIGURE 8.1 Number of employees in selected international organizations.
(*Source: Yearbook* of the United Nations, various years).

difficulties because the international organizations have an incentive to hide rapid growth in the number of their staff. Nevertheless the datas available suffice for illustrative purposes.

The number of staff employed by the International Labour Organization (ILO) and the International Atomic Energy Agency (IAEA) nicely fits the theoretic propositions (the decrease in the number of personal 1975–77 is due to the United States leaving ILO which lead to a strong reduction in the contributions). For the Food and Agriculture Organization (FAO) there is no single time series for the whole period available; obviously the figures since 1973 (except the one for 1975) belong to a series which is systematically lower than the one in use before 1973. The combination of the two again indicates a remarkable growth in the number of staff from around 4000 in 1963 to 7500 in 1980, an increase of 83 per cent.

EXTERNAL ACTIVITIES:
THE EXAMPLE OF THE WORLD BANK

The typical internal features of international organizations, combined with the setting of constraints within which they act, make it possible to derive testable propositions about their external behaviour. Specifically, the World Bank is considered here.

The World Bank is composed of the International Bank for Reconstruction and Development (IBRD) and the International Development Association (IDA). Both institutions have been created to extend credits for economic development. When Third World countries complained that the IBRD was insisting too much on commercial terms of credit, the IDA was founded specially to give credits to developing countries on more favourable terms.

COMPETING MODELS

Four models of World Bank behaviour are compared: (1) where credits are extended to those countries that 'need' them most ('needs model'); (2) where credits are given to those countries that 'deserve' them most ('deserts model'); (3) where the World Bank is run by benevolent officials acting in accordance with the officially stated goals ('benevolence model'); (4) where the World Bank is considered to be a bureaucracy which furthers the utility of its members, subject to economic and political constraints ('politico-economic model').

1   The *needs model* stipulates that the World Bank extends most of its credits to those countries that are in greatest need of such financial aid. It is expected that credits will be the higher, the lower the income per capita is (which, of course, is highly correlated with indicators of poverty such as food or calory intake). The need for financial support is reflected further in other indicators, in particular the rate of inflation (showing the internal strain of demand on real resources), and the accumulated external debt (showing the strain of demand on foreign resources). On the other hand, surpluses in the balance of payments and/or government's budget would be held as signs of minor neediness.

Table 8.2, col. (2), shows the expected signs of the parameters of the five causal variables just discussed on the per capita amount of credits received.

2   The *deserts model* starts from the premise that those countries get most credits from the World Bank that deserve them most. Countries that have made the strongest efforts to develop themselves are therefore expected to get the most financial aid. This means that economically and financially 'responsible' (past) policies are rewarded by the Bank. This 'responsibility' is reflected in a country's low rate of inflation (indicating that the government is determined not to resort to financially unsound policies), a surplus in the balance of payments) demonstrating a prudent import policy and/or successful export policy), a low external debt (showing that the country makes its development effort on its own), and a budget surplus (implying that government is thrifty). A country also deserves credits if its growth in the past has been high (proving that it is capable of development). Finally, a 'responsible' policy also implies that the government is successful in maintaining social peace and political stability, which can be measured by a low number of politically caused strikes and riots.

Table 8.2, col. (3), lists the expected parameter signs for the effect of these causal variables on World Bank credits.

3 According to the *benevolence model*, the officials of the World Bank are 'benevolent bureaucrats', fulfilling their task of following the officially declared goals for the organization. IBRD and IDA have the same basic objectives. Article I of the Articles of Agreement of IDA, effective since 24 September 1960, states the following Purposes (see Mason and Asher 1973, p. 788):

> The purposes of the Association are to promote economic development, increase productivity and thus raise standards of living in the less-developed areas . . . in particular by providing finance to meet their important developmental requirements on terms which are more flexible and bear less heavily on the balance of payments than those of conventional loans . . .

This may be interpreted to mean that developing countries running a structural balance of payments deficit and thus having a high external debt would, *ceteris paribus*, receive more credits than countries that are in a more fortunate situation. The goal of promoting economic development means that countries that have a low per capita income and have experienced low growth in the past will have more credits extended to them by the Bank. According to article 1, III of the Charter, the Bank's goal is to promote the expansion of international trade. In the absence of reliable data on the great many forms of import restrictions, a country's willingness to benefit from the advantages of international trade and investment, measured by the foreign investment climate, may be taken. According to this model, it is to be expected that the more credits will be forthcoming the more 'capitalist' a country is.

Table 8.2, col. (4), shows the parameter signs expected on the basis of the benevolence model.

4 The *politico-economic model* posits that the World Bank must be regarded as a bureaucracy in which the individual members (the employees) further their own utility, subject to various constraints. The utility is composed of the prestige within the banking community, the discretionary power *vis-à-vis* donor and recipient governments, and the maintenance of a political attitude biased to the right (owing to the fact that the professional

staff is heavily dominated by American, British and continental European personnel).

Prestige can be gained within the banking community by 'performance excellence', i.e. by showing that the organization's tasks are competently handled. This means in particular that those countries receive the most credits that have a low per capita income and have shown themselves to be worthy of assistance by having grown rapidly in the past. Discretionary power can be ensured and increased by minimizing the probability and intensity of intervention, especially by donor countries. Governments have, in fact, few incentives to interfere directly with the Bank's daily business because such action is likely to provoke conflicts with other nations, except when the Bank can be accused of having made a serious error. The officials of the World Bank are therefore strongly interested in avoiding major blunders, which induces them to avoid risks. Countries with high external debts and unstable political conditions will accordingly be given less credit, since both features make future defaults more likely. Similarly, a government's budget deficit and a balance of payments deficit will decrease the official's willingness to extend credits, since they make the repayment of the loans harder to achieve. The right-wing political attitudes are served by taking low inflation as an important prerequisite for receiving credits (this also fully accords with the views of the banking community) and by favouring countries with a 'capitalist' orientation.

The most important constraint imposed on the behaviour of the World Bankers is the interference of the donor countries, exerted mainly through their voting rights in the governing bodies, but also through more informal channels. The donor countries tend to intervene in favour of those developing countries that depend on them. Metropolitan countries will support the interests of their former colonies or of countries they dominated in cultural, political and economic ways. This applies in particular to the former large colonial powers, the UK and France, as well as to the LDCs dominated by the United States. It is thus expected that former colonies or dominions of these three countries, *ceteris paribus*, get more credits than the other countries.

The World Bank officials are, of course, also subject to financial constraints. However, this has already been provided for

TABLE 8.2   World bank credits: causal variables, theoretically expected parameter signs for the four models, and econometrically measured parameter signs

	Parameter signs*					
	Theoretically expected for the models				Econometrically estimated for the dependent variables:	
Causal variables (1)	Needs (2)	Deserts (3)	Benevolence (4)	Politico-economic (5)	IBRD loans (6)	IDA credits (7)
Economic variables						
(1) Per capita income	−	0	−	−	−	−
(2) Rate of inflation	+	−	0	−	−	−
(3) Balance of payments surplus	−	+	−	+	+	n.s.
(4) Budget surplus	−	+	0	+	+	n.s.
(5) External debt	+	−	+	−	+	+
(6) Past growth	0	+	−	+	+	+
Political variables						
(7) Political instability	0	−	0	−	−	n.s.
(8) 'Capitalist' climate	0	0	+	+	+	n.s.
Dependency variables Former colonies and dominions of						
(9) United Kingdom	0		0	+	+	n.s.
(10) France	0		0	+	+	+
(11) United States				+	+	+

*+means that the parameter sign is positive, − that it is negative, 0 that it is expected to be *zero*; n.s. implies that the estimated parameter sign is not statistically significant.

Source: Frey and Schneider (1984)

INTERNATIONAL ORGANIZATIONS

TABLE 8.3   Cross-section analysis of world bank credits: IBRD loans
to 60 developing countries; average over the period 1972–81, and IDA

		Economic variables					
		Income per capita (t-2)	*Inflation rate* (t-2)	*Balance of paym. per capita* (t-2)	*Budget surplus; share of GNP* (t-2)	*External debt per capita* (t-2)	*Growth of GNP* (t-2)
Dependent variable	*Constant term*	(1)	(2)	(3)	(4)	(5)	(6)
IBRD loans							
(per capita) (a)	5.04	−0.57**	−0.22*	0.23*	0.12$^{(*)}$	0.15**	0.64**
	(1.31)	(−2.87)	(−2.48)	(2.62)	(1.72)	(2.93)	(3.47)
		−0.28	−0.08	0.32	0.08	0.29	0.26
IDA credits							
(comm. per	5.98	−0.39**	−0.11*	0.04	0.01	0.05*	1.16**
capita) (a)	(1.59)	(−3.12)	(−2.04)	(0.69)	(0.94)	(2.17)	(2.83)
		−0.65	−0.12	0.01	0.02	0.39	0.31

* The independent economic, political, and dependency variables are averaged over the period 1970–9:
i.e. a two-year lag is chosen, as it is assumed that the World Bank officials need two years time to react
and change policies towards developing countries; OLS-regressions: the figures in parentheses below
the estimated coefficients are the t-values are the β-coefficients; an asterisk in parentheses means that
the variable has a significant influence at the 90% level of confidence; one asterisk indicates that the
variable has a significant influence at the 95% level, and two asterisks at the 99% level of confidence

by the risk-averse behaviour described above, which reduces the
chance of default, and by the willingness of the Bank's bureaucrats to yield to the pressure of donor countries, thereby securing
the future flow of contributions to the funds.

Table 8.2, col. (5), lists the signs expected for the parameters
on the basis of the politico-economic model.

Table 8.2, cols (2)-(5), gives a general view of, and allows a comparison between, the theoretically expected effects of the causal
variables (col. 1) on the size of the World Bank credits, according
to the four models discussed. As may be seen, the models' predictions differ significantly from each other both with respect to the
causal variables included and with respect to the expected signs of
the parameters. The needs model is restricted to purely economic
explanatory variables; the deserts model incorporates one political variable (political instability), as does the benevolence model
('capitalist' climate); the politico-economic model takes into
account both political and dependency variables.

credits (commitments) to 48 developing countries; average over the period 1972–81*

Political variables		Dependency variables			Test statistics			
Political instability† (t-2) (7)	Capitalist climate (t-2) (8)	Colonies and dominions						
		UK (9a)	Fr. (10a)	USA (11a)	$\bar{R}^2$	F_{all}	F_{dy}	d.f.
−0.21[(*)]	3.54*	1.84[(*)]	4.99*	1.94*	0.64	7.09	4.64	47
(−1.79)	(2.16)	(1.89)	(2.61)	(2.12)				
−0.09	0.21	0.18	0.43	0.28				
−0.46	1.85	1.06	3.86**	1.46*	0.54	6.53	4.21	35
(−1.61)	(0.89)	(1.27)	(2.89)	(2.13)				
−0.17	0.06	0.10	0.44	0.20				

(all three: two-tailed tests); $\bar{R}^2$ is the coefficient of determination corrected for degrees of freedom; F_{all} (F_{dy}) indicates whether in total the independent (all-dummy) variables have a significant impact on the dependent variable.
† The political variable 'political instability' is averaged only over the period 1970–77; after 1977 no data were available.
Source: Frey and Schneider (1984).

ESTIMATION RESULT

The four models were econometrically tested with data for 60 less developed countries receiving credits. The dependent variables are IBRD loans and IDA commitments in US$ per capita, averaged over the period 1972–81. Two equations each have been estimated with the ordinary least squares method for IBRD loans and for IDA credits. The regression results are presented in table 8.3.

The equations are statistically satisfactory. They account for 64 and 54 per cent of the variance, and the $\hat{F}$-test indicates that the set of explanatory variables has a significant influence on World Bank credits (99 per cent level of security). A large number of the parameters is significantly different from zero at the 90, 95 and 99 per cent levels of security.

In general, the estimates indicate that World Bank credits are influenced not only by economic variables (1)–(6), but also by the political variables (7)–(8) and the dependency variables (9)–(11).

An application of the $\hat{F}$-test for the set of variables (9)–(11) indicates that dependency has a statistically significant influence on World Bank credits at the 99 per cent level of security.

The qualitative results of the econometric estimates are tabulated in columns (6) and (7) of table 8.2, allowing a direct comparison with the signs theoretically expected on the basis of the four models. The needs model correctly forecasts the direction of influence of income (negative) and external debt (positive) on credits, but incorrectly predicts that, *ceteris paribus*, a higher rate of inflation, a balance of payments deficit and a budget deficit (at least for IBRD loans) will help to secure more credits, whereas the econometric estimates suggest the contrary. The needs model does not make any prediction about the influence of past growth, whereas the empirical estimates find that it contributes to more credits. Concerning the political and dependency variables, the model again suggests that they do not have any influence; the empirical results indicate that both the 'capitalist' climate and political instability (for IBRD loans), as well as being a British or French ex-colony or a US ex-dependency, help to obtain more credits. The needs model correctly predicts that having been a British colony does not affect the credits granted by IDA from the World Bank. Table 8.4, col. (2), summarizes these results for the needs model for the case of IBRD loans: 2 parameter signs are correctly predicted, in 6 cases a statistically significant influence was not predicted, and 3 parameters have the wrong sign compared with the estimates.

The deserts model has a superior overall performance (compare cols. (3) and (2) in table 8.4), and it differs in several respects from the needs model; in particular, the sole erroneously predicted parameter sign is that an increasing external debt would, *ceteris paribus*, reduce credits, while the econometric estimates suggest that this contributes to receiving higher credits.

The benevolence model is able to predict 3 parameters correctly and 2 incorrectly (col. (4) of table 8.4). Again, the pattern of 'hits' and 'misses' is different from the other two models just discussed. Among the political variables, the predicted insignificant effect of political instability on credits is correct only for IDA credits.

The politico-economic model makes the largest number of

TABLE 8.4   The performance of the four competing models:
comparison of the theoretically expected and the empirically estimated
parameters, for IBRD loans

(1)	Theoretical models			
	Needs (2)	*Deserts* (3)	*Benevolence* (4)	*Politico-economic* (5)
Correct sign	2	5	3	10
No influence expected while there is an empirically significant sign, or the reverse	6	5	6	0
Wrong sign	3	1	2	1

Derived from table 8.2, and explained in the text.

Source: Frey and Schneider (1984).

predictions about whether an influence should run in the positive
or negative direction. The model predicts incorrectly that increasing external debt makes it difficult to get more credits, but
predicts correctly the direction of influence with respect to 10
causal variables, including many of the political and dependency
effects.

A comparison of the performance of the four models as
compiled in table 8.4 suggests that the politico-economic model is
superior to the others, having a significantly higher number of
correct predictions and a lower number of incorrect ones. The
politico-economic model thus provides us with the greatest
amount of useful information about the World Bank's lending
activity, and leads us less often than the other models into a
wrong direction.

CONCLUSION

The functioning of international organizations is strongly determined by the voting rule applied. The unanimity rule is used to
secure the support of all countries involved, but tends to lead to

slow and ill-suited decisions. Majority voting appears most often in the form of weighted and qualified rules, which enable the more important and more strongly affected countries to be given a greater say in the decisions. There is a variety of new voting rules, such as voting by veto or the preference-revealing mechanism. Given the vote shares of a country and the decision rule in force, it is possible to derive, *a priori* a measure of the relative power of the nation within an international organization by considering how often the country casts the decisive vote. An increase in the vote share may under some circumstances lead to a decrease in relative power. However, this power index is able to capture only limited aspects of a country's influence.

Internally, international organizations show the characteristics of bureaucratic behaviour in an extreme way, because in the absence of an incentive to control them by national governments they have considerable discretionary leeway. This is shown, for example, by a considerable portion of the budget being devoted to internal purposes.

The external behaviour of international organizations has been illustrated for the World Bank. Four competing models have been constructed. Econometric tests indicate that the politico-economic model performs best, which suggests that, in addition to economic factors such as per capita income, inflation, balance of payments deficit, budget deficit, external debt and past growth, one has to include political factors such as the 'capitalist' climate or political instability arising from strikes and riots. The results also suggest that the economic, cultural and political influences that are due to the former status of the recipient country as a colony or dominion are important, at least for France and the United States.

FURTHER READING

WORKS CITED IN THE TEXT

Brams, Steven J. (1976), *Paradoxes in Politics*. London: Macmillan.

Cairncross, Alec, Giersch, Herbert, Lamfalussy, Alexandre, Petrelli, Guiseppe and Uri, Pierre (1974), *Wirtschaftspolitik für Europa*. München: Piper.

Dreyer, Jacob S., and Schotter, Andrew (1980), 'Power Relationships in the International Monetary Fund. The Consequences of Quota Changes'. *Review of Economics and Statistics*, 62 (February), 97–106.

Faber, Malte, and Breyer, Friedrich (1980), 'Eine ökonomische Analyse konstitutioneller Aspekte der europäischen Integration'. *Jahrbuch für Sozialwissenschaft*, 31, 213–27.

Frey, Bruno S. (1983), *Democratic Economic Policy*. Oxford: Martin Robertson.

Frey, Bruno S. and Schneider, Friedrich (1984), 'Competing Models of International Lending Activity'. Institute of Empirical Economic Research, University of Zurich. Mimeo.

Mason, Edward S., and Asher, Robert E. (1973), *The World Bank since Bretton Woods*. Washington DC: Brookings Institution.

Mueller, Dennis C. (1978), 'Voting by Veto'. *Journal of Public Economics*, 10 (August), 57–75.

Tideman, T. Nicolaus, and Tullock, Gordon (1976), 'A New and Superior Process for Making Social Choices'. *Journal of Political Economy*, 84 (December), 1145–59.

WORKS RELATING TO OTHER ASPECTS DISCUSSED

For factual information and further literature on international organizations see, for example,

McBean, Alasdair and Snowden, Nicholas (1981), *International Institutions in Trade and Finance*. London: Allen & Unwin.

van Meerhaege, M.A.G. (1980), *A Handbook of International Economic Institutions*. The Hague: Martinus Nijhoff.

Voting rules are discussed in

Mueller, Dennis C. (1979), *Public Choice*. Cambridge: Cambridge University Press.

Factual information is given by

Zamora, Stephen (1980), 'Voting in International Economic Organizations'. *American Journal of International Law*, 74 (July), 566–608.

The economic theory of bureaucracy used to analyse internal behaviour is the topic of

Breton, Albert, and Wintrobe, Ronald (1982), *The Logic of Bureaucratic Conduct*. Cambridge: Cambridge University Press.

9

What Have We Learnt?

THE MAIN PROBLEM AREAS

International political economics deals with the interplay of economic and political aspects in the international sphere. The book has presented various areas in which such interactions take place.

PROTECTIONISM

Most attention has been focused on the study of tariff formation, which demonstrates well the application of the economic approach in explaining pressing problems of the international economy.

International political economics endeavours to reveal the forces that determine whether a particular branch of a national economy is highly or only weakly protected. This goal differs basically from the traditional theory of international trade, which either takes tariffs as given and analyses the effects they have on the national and international economy, or decides what tariffs would be socially optimal provided there is a 'benevolent dictator' capable and willing to put such an optimal tariff into reality.

Actual tariffs are determined by the demand for, and supply of, protection on a political market. Capital owners, management and workers of import-competing industries unite to lobby for higher tariffs because the resulting increase in domestic prices yields them a rent which they can distribute among themselves. The pro-tariff interests are often well organized (there is usually only a small number of relevant suppliers in any particular industry), and their demand for protection against the 'cut-throat' competition from abroad has political appeal among the population and politicians. Econometric evidence (mainly for the United States, but also for other countries) indicates that the drive for protection will be the more successful, the more concentrated the industry is (which facilitates interest group organization). The same applies to declining industries, and sectors with a large number of low-wage employees (which gives more credibility to the demand for protection). It is the consumer sector that would benefit most from low tariffs and increased competition by foreign suppliers; owing to their vast size and fragmentation, however, they are not able to counterbalance the pro-tariff demands of the import-competing domestic suppliers.

Protectionism does not only take the form of tariffs; there are many other means of impairing competition from foreign suppliers, the most important of which is the qualitative import restrictions and administrative regulations imposing special burdens on imports. Empirical estimates for the United States suggest that such non-tariff barriers are used by protectionist groups not only to substitute for general reductions in tariffs (agreed on in international negotiations such as the Kennedy or Tokyo Rounds) but also to complement tariffs. While strongly concentrated and therefore well organized and politically powerful industries are well able to influence tariffs, less concentrated industries see better chances in lobbying for non-tariff barriers, because the rents generated from protection can often be distributed selectively so as to motivate domestic suppliers to take part in setting forth the political demands. Voluntary export restraints (which are compatible with GATT agreements on trade liberalization) are an especially attractive form of protection for the major organized groups of domestic suppliers, the national government and public bureaucracy, as well as for the foreign suppliers, who can appropriate the rents created by the price increase brought about by the supply restrictions. The losers are the little organized and little informed consumers.

International political economics can also throw light on how protectionism varies over time: in the downturn of the business cycle, the high rate of unemployment strengthens the political position of the protectionist interests, which induces the government to increase tariffs and other protective devices. On the other hand, when inflation rises in a booming period and the population considers this an evil, a vote-dependent government is motivated to encourage foreign competition in an effort therewith to reduce inflationary pressure.

The study of protectionism illustrates well how the economic way of thinking is applied to problems of international political economy. It has become clear not only that it is the jargon of economics (such as 'demand' and 'supply') that is used, but also that the underlying behaviour of individuals and groups is carefully analysed. The uniform methodological approach allows us to consider actions simultaneously in the economic and the political spheres.

FOREIGN DIRECT INVESTMENT

Multinational enterprises are prepared to provide both the capital and the entrepreneurial knowledge (i.e. to invest directly) in a developing country if they can expect a positive return, compared with alternative investment outlets. This expected return depends on both economic and political conditions in the countries to be invested in. An LDC will attract more foreign direct investment the higher its real per capita GNP and the lower its balance of payments deficit. Somewhat less important are a high growth of GNP and the availability of a skilled labour force. On the other hand, high inflation and high wage costs are economic factors reducing direct foreign investment.

One of the most important political factors influencing the expected rates of return of multinational firms is political risk. Empirical studies suggest that the risk of being expropriated or of being forced to divest (without adequate compensation) is not so large as often thought, and that this risk differs strongly between the sectors invested in. It is shown, however, that risk in the form of political instability does significantly reduce foreign direct investment, and that an LDC attracts more of such investment the more bilateral and multilateral aid the LDC receives. The host government's political ideology is of little importance, as it does not directly affect the expected returns of carefully planning multinational firms.

FOREIGN AID

The amount of official aid given by an industrial country to a
developing country is decided to a large extent by the government
and its bureaucracy, because neither voters nor interest groups
have a strong and persistent interest in this particular issue. The
discretionary room accorded to the politicians and public officials
is used to further their own goals, in particular to undertake a
desired foreign policy. To promote their country's international
standing yields benefits to members of a government and public
officials in terms of prestige, and possibly influence, in the
diplomatic world. A recipient country can actively influence the
amount of aid received by choosing an appropriate political
position *vis-à-vis* the donor country. An LDC that always or
never aligns with the donor (for example with respect to voting in
the UN) is likely to receive less aid than one that makes it clear
that it will be prepared to support the donor's position in return
for financial aid. The interrelationship becomes more complex if
two competing donors and one recipient country are considered.
The amount of aid, and the distribution of its sources, then
depends on whether the donors are prepared to tolerate a
neutralist position, and on whether the LDC has a preference for
a particular position on international issues or simply wishes to
maximize the amount of aid received.

Empirical evidence suggests that a donor country tends to react
when the amount of aid given by other donors is increased
because it is afraid of losing influence. In such a situation, foreign
aid is increased to check the other donors' influence. Foreign aid
is therefore no 'international public good'; rather, the LDCs
benefit from the aid competition among donors.

TRADE WARS

Boycotts are used to disrupt trade and finance in order to
influence the targeted country's political position. Such economic
sanctions have rarely proved effective because the necessary
administrative, economic and political conditions have not been
met. One of the main reasons why economic sanctions generally

do not work is that the production and consumption patterns of the boycotted nations are quite flexible, so that an adjustment is possible and imports and exports can be undertaken via nations not participating in the sanctions, or by illegal trade which opens up in response to the high profit opportunities created. Moreover, the administration of the sanctions by the boycotting nation or nations is usually slow and leaves sufficient leaks to allow the targeted country to remain relatively unharmed. Finally, the political reaction in the boycotted country may be counterproductive, tending to raise nationalist feelings and thereby to cripple the opposition against the government. At least in the short run, this cements the political position taken so far.

Economic sanctions are costly to the nation(s) imposing them because benefits from international trade are given up, and competing suppliers may instead establish themselves in the market. Despite these costs, and the probable ineffectiveness of trade wars, governments are often compelled to engage in them because they constitute the only means available short of inaction (which the population would not tolerate in most circumstances) or military war.

INTERNATIONAL CO-OPERATION

Sovereign nations have great problems in protecting global common property resources and establishing mutually beneficial rules and instructions. Important areas are international military alliances (such as NATO), international monetary agreements (such as the Bretton Woods system) and international natural resources (such as fishing stock and minerals contained in the oceans). Each nation has an incentive to free-ride in the presence of such international public goods. Co-operation can be attained by transforming the international public good into national (private) goods so that a country finds it individually worthwhile to participate in the conservation. This is usually achieved by a sequential bargaining process on a quasi-market in which the private goods are exchanged, and trust among the participating nations slowly emerges.

Another possibility for reaching international co-operation is to establish a constitutional agreement in which the rules governing the interaction among the nations are set down. Voluntary co-operation will come about only if the participating countries expect such an agreement to be profitable for themselves over the (partly unknown) future. The smaller the number of countries involved, the more likely it is that such a mutually beneficial agreement can be reached, because free-riding is less possible.

INTERNATIONAL ORGANIZATIONS

National governments have few incentives or opportunities to monitor the behaviour of the international organizations to which they belong. Such organizations therefore have considerable discretionary power and show the characteristic traits of bureaucracies. A considerable part of the discretionary leeway is used for the benefits of the international public officials themselves, or results in red tape, such as the production of memoranda and papers for purely internal purposes. Another result is that international bureaucracies tend to grow quite independently of the tasks initially assigned to them, and/or start to define their tasks themselves. Empirical evidence suggests that international organizations tend to increase rapidly in terms of employees and administrative budget. The role played by the member-countries depends strongly on the voting rule in force. An *a priori* measure of relative power can be derived on the basis of the vote shares of the individual countries and the particular voting rule, by determining how often a country is able to cast the decisive vote. However, this power index is able to identify only limited aspects of a country's influence within an international organization.

The behaviour of international organizations can be analysed by econometric methods. The World Bank's distribution of credits among the LDCs is an example. A developing country *ceteris paribus* gets more credits the lower its per capita real income and the higher its external (public) debt. These two factors indicate that LDCs in particularly unfortunate economic circumstances get more credits from the World Bank. The empirical evidence also shows, however, that the higher the rate of inflation, and the larger the balance of payments and budget deficits, the *fewer* credits are received. This suggests that the World Bank is a bureaucratic organization whose members pursue policies furthering their own utility. They win the applause of the banking community (which is their main reference group) if they behave in a risk-averse and financially conservative way by extending credits mainly to countries with strict monetary and fiscal policies (as revealed by low inflation and low balance of payments and budget deficits). The risk aversion and financial and political conservatism of world bankers is also reflected in the extension of higher credits to countries with a 'capitalist' climate and stable political conditions (that is, few strikes and riots). In order to minimize possible conflicts with the main financial contributors, the world bankers tend to favour (under otherwise equal economic and political conditions) former colonies and dominions of these nations. This political influence shows in particular in the case of LDCs formerly connected with either France or the United States.

EVALUATION

The international politico-economic interactions have been analysed using the approach and the methodological tools of modern economics. International political economics may be considered as the part of modern political economy that applies the economic approach to politics in general. It does, however, sometimes transcend the limits of public choice narrowly conceived, which identifies economic theory totally with orthodox neoclassics and leaves no room for other elements.

The economic approach to the study of international politico-economic relations has both strengths and weaknesses.

STRENGTHS

Without doubt, one of the great assets of international political economics is its emphasis on *human behaviour*. While the relationships studied may sometimes be abstract, they gain life by the fact that they do not exist in isolation but are always the result of human action. The actions taken are attributed to individuals pursuing their own advantage within the constraints imposed by other actors, by institutions and by the scarcity of resources. Individuals take their decisions by comparing the benefits and costs of the alternatives open to them. They are assumed to be rational in the (limited) sense that they are able to perform such an evaluation and to draw the correct conclusions therefrom, in such a way that there is a systematic and hence predictable relationship between the expected net benefits and the behaviour revealed. It is, however, in no way assumed that the individuals are fully informed. It has been pointed out in various instances that under some circumstances the individuals have little incentive to be well informed. One example is that the voters are little interested in, and therefore collect and evaluate little information, about, foreign aid.

It should have become clear that the economists' methodological individualism does not mean that individuals are the only actors considered. Indeed, actions have often been attributed to groups of individuals (e.g. to interest groups lobbying for protection) or to organizations (e.g. to the government, or even to countries in the care of donors and recipients of foreign aid). If there is a sufficient amount of homogeneity within such aggregates it is useful to use them as the acting units as long as one is prepared to relate the actions to individual actors if deemed necessary.

This emphasis on human behaviour as the driving force behind international politico-economic relations is in stark contrast to the political scientists' international political economy, which largely abstracts from human action and tends to stress functional relationships.

Another major strength of international political economics is its *explicit analysis of institutions*. Throughout the book the institutional conditions existing have played a major role in the analysis. 'Institutions' have been understood in a broad sense, covering decision-making mechanisms (e.g. democratic voting by citizens and bargaining by interest groups about tariffs and other trade restrictions), explicit and implicit rules (e.g. concerning the use of global common property resources) and organizations (such as the World Bank).

The analysis of institutions sets international political economics strongly apart from the 'pure' theory of international trade, which explicitly considers only one sole institution, the price system or market (see Schotter 1981). This is one of the main reasons why orthodox international economics is considered by many students as well as researchers as a rather bloodless, abstract and possibly rather irrelevant endeavour. International political economics is also quite distinct from 'applied' international economics. In contrast to this field (which is concerned in particular with monetary aspects), the working of the institutions is not simply described, but analysed. Theoretical propositions are derived that can be put to an empirical test. This has, for example, been done for the case of the World Bank.

This leads to a third major strength of international political economics, the *integration of economics and politics*. This is made possible because one methodological approach is applied to the economic and the political spheres. As has become apparent in the discussion of, for instance, the factors determining foreign direct investment or the conditions necessary for economic sanctions to be effective, individuals, groups and organizations are assumed to pursue their goals simultaneously by economic and political means, and are subject to both economic and political constraints.

SHORTCOMINGS AND DANGERS

While the model of behaviour forming the basis of international political economics is valuable and may well be considered superior to corresponding models in political science or sociology, it is in no way fully developed. One of the main shortcomings is that typically human traits are not sufficiently considered. Indeed, the model of utility maximization subject to constraints has been successfully used to explain the behaviour of animals (pigeons, rats) in laboratory experiments (see Battalio et al. 1981). It may be argued that man is distinguished from animals in his capacity to ponder about his preferences (Hirschman 1982). Recently there have been various attempts to introduce such notions into the analysis (e.g. Sen 1982; Margolis 1982). In particular, the concept of meta-preference, or preference about one's preferences, has been introduced. This takes into account the fact that individuals may be dissatisfied with their present preferences (for instance, they would wish not to prefer to smoke or eat too much). They then resort to all kinds of tricks against themselves in order not to fall prey to their unwanted desires (cigarettes are put in a place that is difficult to reach, etc.) Such a pre-commitment was used by Ulysses, who, knowing of the dangers of the sirens, ordered his companions to bind him to the mast and not to release him under any circumstances. This and other extensions further increase the realism of the model of human behaviour and may also help us more easily to grasp certain phenomena in international political economy.

Another shortcoming of the economic approach to international politico-economic relations is the somewhat loose relationship between the theoretical propositions developed and the empirical analysis undertaken. This is, for instance, apparent in the econometric tests of the positive theory of protectionism. The multiple regressions often test not the theoretical propositions, but some indirect consequences thereof. A vote-dependent government's need to please the electorate by an appropriate protectionist policy over the course of the business cycle, for instance, is econometrically analysed by running a multiple time-series regression of unemployment and inflation on some indicator of the degree of protectionism. The result of such an empirical analysis is compatible with a number of rather distinct theories. A better test of the underlying theory would require an explicit model of government and voter behaviour, of the economic relationships over the cycle, as well as of the impact of changes in protection on the domestic economy. For that purpose, the work undertaken in the politico-economic modelling of closed economies (see e.g. the articles collected in Hibbs and Fassbender 1981, or in Whiteley 1980) may be used.

A third shortcoming of the works discussed in international political economics is that they do not (or insufficiently) consider the closed-loop interdependence of the economy and policy. So far, the main emphasis has been rightly put on explaining the politico-economic nature of aspects neglected in traditional international economics. Thus, the object of study has been the political and economic influences on tariffs and other forms of protection, on foreign direct investment and on foreign aid. The next step is to integrate the economic effects thereby brought about. When protection against foreign competition is changed, and when there is a changing inflow of foreign aid and foreign direct investment, the economies concerned are of course affected, which in turn influences the politico-economic decisions. It may, for instance, be hypothesized that, when foreign direct investment leads to a rise in national income of the recipient country, political risk is reduced, leading to a further inflow of foreign direct investment. Knowledge about the economic repercussions mentioned is derived from traditional international economics.

It is thus clear that the conventional and the politico-economic theories of international economics have to supplement each other. It should be added that the fact that these wider causal interdependencies should be taken into account in future work does not mean that the estimates presented in this book are biased (in the statistical sense). Simultaneous econometric estimation techniques are necessary only if the interdependencies are not subject to time lags. It can as a rule be assumed that the decision-making and the economic effects take some time to occur, so that the underlying model is of a recursive nature. Experience, moreover, shows that the more complicated simultaneous estimation techniques often yield results quite similar to more simple approaches.

OUTLOOK

The discussion should have made clear that the shortcomings of international political economics as it exists today can be overcome by carefully extending the theoretical concepts and models used. There is another danger that has to be faced: in economics as well as in public choice there is a certain tendency for each field of enquiry to become increasingly formal, and to lose touch with reality. This danger can be checked by linking theoretical and empirical research closely together, as has been endeavoured in this book. International political economics has already provided many interesting and novel insights into the interplay of economics and politics in the international sphere. It presents a useful and even indispensable complement to traditional international economics, as well as to the political scientists' approaches. In this book only selected areas have been presented; it is left to the reader to think of other areas of international politico-economic relations that could be fruitfully dealt with. There is little doubt that there are many.

FURTHER READING

WORKS CITED IN THE TEXT

Battalio, Raymond C., Kegel, John H., Racklin, Howard, and Green, Leonard (1981), 'Commodity Choice Behaviour with Pigeons as Subjects'. *Journal of Political Economy*, 84 (February), 116–51.

Hibbs, Douglas A., and Fassbender, Heino (eds) (1981), *Contemporary Political Economy*. Amsterdam: North Holland.

Hirschman, Albert O. (1982), *Shifting Involvements. Private Interest and Public Action*. Oxford: Martin Robertson.

Margolis, Howard (1982), *Selfishness, Altruism, and Rationality. A Theory of Social Choice*. Cambridge: Cambridge University Press.

Schotter, Andrew (1981), *The Economic Theory of Social Institutions*. Cambridge: Cambridge University Press.

Sen, Amartya K. (1982), 'Rational Fools: A Critique of the Behavioural Foundations of Economic Theory'. In Amartya K. Sen, *Choice, Welfare and Measurement*. Oxford: Basil Blackwell, 84-107

Whiteley, Paul (ed.) (1980), *Models of Political Economy*. London and Beverly Hills: Sage.

WORKS RELATING TO OTHER ASPECTS DISCUSSED

Simple, but instructive applications of the economic model of behaviour are provided in

Tullock, Gordon, and McKenzie, Richard (1975), *The New World of Economics*. London: Irwin.

Limits of the economic model of man revealed by laboratory experiments are discussed by

Kahneman, Daniel and Tversky, Amos (1979), 'Prospect Theory: An Analysis of Decision under Risk'. *Econometrica* 47, 263–91.

Fascinating extensions of the model of human behaviour are also suggested by

Elster, Jon (1979), *Ulysses and the Sirens. Studies in Rationality and Irrationality*. Cambridge: Cambridge University Press.

Schelling, Thomas (1980), 'The Intimate Contest for Self-command? *Public Interest* 60 (Summer), 94–118.

Other particularly important, earlier, contributions are

Simon, Herbert A. (1957), *Models of Man*. New York: John Wiley.

Scitovsky, Tibor (1976), *The Joyless Economy: An Inquiry into Human Satisfaction and Consumer Dissatisfaction*. Oxford: Oxford University Press.

Politico-economic models of closed economies have recently been developed by

Borooah, Vani K., and van der Ploeg, Frederick (1983), *Political Aspects of the Economy*. Cambridge: Cambridge University Press.

van Winden, Frans (1983), *On the Interaction between State and Private Sector*. Amsterdam: North Holland.

Author Index

Subject Index